T0110614

YOU HAVE THE POWER

To Fully Recover From Your Alcohol Use Disorder

No Steps Required

Joseph R. Rizza

authorHOUSE®

AuthorHouse™
1663 Liberty Drive
Bloomington, IN 47403
www.authorhouse.com
Phone: 833-262-8899

Published by AuthorHouse 03/04/2022

ISBN: 978-1-6655-5277-6 (sc)
ISBN: 978-1-6655-5278-3 (e)

Library of Congress Control Number: 2022903372

Print information available on the last page.

This book is printed on acid-free paper.

CONTENTS

Life in the Present Moment

Your Happiness

Happiness Strategies

A Summary

A Glossary

INTRODUCTION

Rewinding time is not possible...but *do-overs* are.

You decide every moment of every day, who you are and
what you believe in.

You get a second chance...every second.

Never let the sadness of your past or the fear of your future
ruin the happiness of your present.

Life is all about second chances...
getting a *re-do,* a *do-over,* a *retry,* a *replay,* a *mulligan.*

Technically...you can't actually *start over,*
but you can *start anew* from right where you are,
from this moment on.

This book that you're reading, was written to
help you to recognize and appreciate the fact that
you (as was I) are being given a second chance...
a chance to live a happy and content life
without the *need* for alcohol.

I strongly urge you to take that chance!

Right now, there are just three things that are required from you —

1 To recognize that you need to *make* a *change* to your lifestyle.

2 To realize that it is *your responsibility* to do so, no one else's.

3 To have the *confidence*, to *believe*, that you can lead a *happy*
and *sober* life.

Change is the act or instance of making something or someone different...to replace one thing with something else...
a modification or transformation.

Only ***you*** can change your life...no one else can do it for you...
the responsibility is yours and yours alone.

Make a conscious decision to take control of your destiny,
confident in your ability to make positive choices
that will result in *you* becoming
a better version of yourself.

"The moment you accept responsibility for
everything in your life is the moment you
gain the power to do anything in your life."
— Hal Elrod

Choosing sobriety is the easy part.

Being committed to an alcohol-free lifestyle is going to require effort on your part (there can be no change without action)
but the benefits will be so worth it...
Your life will improve in a multitude of ways.

Right now, you have two choices: **EVOLVE** OR **REPEAT**

The reason I wrote this book was not for you to *just read it...*
reading is about perusing a topic to gather information...
and while there is nothing wrong with that...

I wrote this book with the hope that you *study* its contents...
devote some time to *understand* the concepts and strategies
as they apply to you.

Please try to keep this book with you at all times...
Treat it like an educational text book...
a *study guide* for your recovery.

My hope for you, is that you become *self-empowered* and
fully recover, as I did...
to do what needs to be done to create your new sober lifestyle
filled with happiness, contentment and inner peace.

Yes, there does exist
the very *real possibility* that
you can **fully recover** from your Alcohol Use Disorder (AUD).

Keep reminding yourself that the reason you are doing this is
to make a better life for yourself.

You are the greatest project you will ever work on.

Second chances are not given to make things right...
they are given to prove that you can *do* better,
you can *be* better, even after you fall.

Life is giving you a second chance...

My advice to you is to —

Take it and

Give it your best shot...Give it all you've got!!!

You CAN Recover and You WILL Recover

Congratulations!!!

You've stopped drinking...Or...
you've sobered up long enough to start reading this book.

Either way, you realized or are beginning to realize, that
drinking excessively wasn't/isn't really working for you.

You are not alone!

It didn't work for me and it really doesn't
work for ANYONE.

You may have started drinking to avoid
a hurt or a pain...
some sorrow or grief...
anxiety...
a worry or
an insecurity.

Most certainly something, or possibly
some things were causing you pain...
preventing you from being happy...
Perhaps, that is why you drank alcohol to an excess.

You drank to temporarily reduce your pain...
to avoid the negativity in your life...
to allow yourself to experience some momentary pleasure,
which your mind mistakenly took for happiness.

You were seeking relief, from an *external* substance,
for an *internal* pain.

Yeah...that really doesn't work!

Over consuming alcohol is a symptom of
discomfort...
a sign that something in your life is
not working and so
you chose to avoid it, because, in some way,
that *something* was/is causing you harm.

You may not even be conscious of this...
but it's true.

I Have Been There!

Addiction arises from your refusal to
face your pain, your insecurity or self-doubt...
so instead,
you used alcohol to numb that pain,
to block out your insecurity or conceal your self-doubt.

And, after the effects of the alcohol wore
off, your unhappiness,
your helplessness,
your dissatisfaction with something in your life returned.

The alcohol didn't reverse your suffering,
and it never will...because it can't.

Right now, you may be feeling a bit
helpless about your situation.

You may even think that *real happiness* for you, is not possible.

But I Can Tell You With Certainty That It Is Possible.

You were *born* with a right to be happy and to enjoy life...
everyone is.

From the moment of your birth,
you were, unknowingly, on a quest for happiness.

Happiness is *your birthright...*

You are *supposed to be* happy...

No one is supposed to be unhappy.

"I believe that the very purpose of life is
happiness...From the very core of our
being, we desire contentment."
— Dalai Lama

But, from the time you were born until now,
so much has happened in your life to affect and
alter your inherent happiness.

The good news is...
You have already begun the process of
regaining or recovering that inherent happiness.

You have taken your first step towards a
happier life by choosing not to drink alcohol
to escape from reality.

You became *aware* of the destructive effects of your
excessive drinking and you put an end to it.

And That, My Friend is a Good Thing!

But now...where do you go from here?

By saying 'NO' to alcohol,
you did something for yourself...
you made a *positive choice.*

However...
the reason why 'Just Saying No' is usually *ineffective*
can be found in that one simple word...'NO'.

It is *ineffective* because the word 'NO'
is associated with a feeling of *rejecting something...*
giving up or
denying yourself something.

So...while just saying "NO" may help to keep you sober,
without making the necessary changes in your life,
It will NOT bring you happiness.

Living your life without alcohol *should not* and
is not about giving something up...
it's not a punishment,
a failure, or
an acceptance of a narrow and restrictive lifestyle.

It is a wise response to an invitation to become
who you were meant to be.

You just need to shift the focus
from what you are denying yourself
to what you are seeking...
Happiness - a sense of well-being, joy and contentment...
being satisfied with your life.

But...
If you don't create a new life for yourself,
making some changes to your lifestyle,
then all the factors that led to your Alcohol Use Disorder (AUD)
will, without a doubt, catch up with you again.

So, in addition to adjusting your drinking habits,
there are some other things you will need to change.

These changes you make, will not all be easy,
but you definitely need to *say goodbye* to your *old lifestyle,*
which brought you to a life of misery and pain.

You need to allow a new identity to emerge...
a life based on positivity, happiness and contentment.

It is time now, for you to *move forward.*

"The secret of change is to focus all of
your energy, not on fighting the old, but
on building the new."
— Socrates

If your aim is to become a person who
doesn't have a *need* to drink alcohol,
then you **must** create for yourself a lifestyle where there is
no valid reason to excessively consume alcohol...
a happy and content life, without a toxic chemical enhancement.

Alcohol is a carcinogenic neurotoxin.
That is why when someone drinks alcohol to an
excess,
they are deemed to be "intoxicated"...
from the Latin word "toxicum" - *to poison.*

Your happiness, as well as your unhappiness,
depends more on your mental state,
(your thoughts, feelings and emotions, your attitude or
your way of thinking)
than by any external happenings, circumstances or experiences.

Whether you are aware of it or not...
YOU actually have the **power,** right now, to create for yourself,
a better and more positive life than you've ever had.

You already have the **power**...You just need to turn it on.

This is no pipe dream...
as the potential to make it come true lies within you.

It is a reality waiting to happen.

Keep in mind that a change will rarely occur
without a new set of conditions...
but I believe you already know that and
that is one of the reasons why you are reading this book.

So it is my hope,
that throughout the pages of this book,
you will find the desire, encouragement and motivation,
the determination
to take this transformational journey
of happiness and contentment...
to finally realize a complete, happy, joyful and content life
without the need or the desire to drink alcohol.

I will tell you from my own personal experience...
IT MOST DEFINITELY CAN BE SO.

"We are what we think. All that arises,
arises with our thoughts.
With our thoughts we make our world."
— Buddha

If you *really believe* that you can, then *indeed* you can.

You are strong enough to face it all,
even if it doesn't feel like it right now...
and there is just one thing you need to know...
one thing you need to remember...

YOU CAN AND YOU WILL RECOVER !!!

One Thing About the Word Recover

To *recover* means to get back or regain something that was taken away from you.

When you hear the word *recover,* you typically think of 'the way you were before your illness'.

Your abuse of alcohol, your excessive drinking, your AUD took you to where you are today.

To *literally recover* would mean to return to the person you were just before you started abusing alcohol.

Just think about it...

If you were to recover that *same* person,
with the *same* thoughts, feelings, emotions, beliefs and behaviors...
what would prevent you from drinking alcohol again?

Why would **this** time be any different?

Was it not those *same* thoughts, emotions and behaviors that led you to your addiction?

I personally, did not want to return to the same person that I was.

I realized that I needed to make some changes to my life...
to make some improvements...
to become a *better version* of myself.

In a sense, I needed to reinvent myself.

To become a better version of yourself,
you will need to make some changes as well.

You do not get over an addiction just by stopping the using.

But you **can recover** by *creating a new life*
where it is *easier* not to drink alcohol to an excess.

If you do not create a new life,
changing your lifestyle,
then all the factors or circumstances that contributed
to your Alcohol Use Disorder will reappear and
lead you back to your previous unhappy,
helpless state.

And I really don't think that is where you want to be.

So when you hear the word *recover* in this book,
please understand it as referring to the **new** you, not the **old** you.

The good news is that
you can completely recover from your Alcohol Use Disorder.

What This Book *is* *NOT* About

This book is *not* a one-size-fits-all program.

There IS no one-size-fits-all approach to sobriety.

It is *not* a Twelve Step program.

In fact...it's *not* a *program* or *regiment* of any kind.

There Are No Rules...
No Steps... only *positive suggestions*,
strategies that have been proven to be effective for
persons in recovery...
but even then, you need not apply or make use of every one.

What works for someone else may not work for you.

This book is *not* about you having a
so-called "incurable disease" of alcoholism.

I firmly believe that Alcoholism or Alcohol Use Disorder (AUD),
as it is now called, is NOT a disease...and you most likely
do *not* have an alleged "alcohol allergy".

The 'disease concept' suggests that a
person who has become abstinent, will be in
perilous remission forever.

That is simply not true!

This book does not suggest that you are
powerless over alcohol.

I did not and
do not believe that I was powerless over alcohol.

I did however, need some help and direction
to begin my recovery and if you are reading this book,
my guess is that you probably do as well.

And the necessary help is what you will get...
that is primarily why I wrote this book...
to share with you,
the things that have helped me to recover from my AUD.

Yes...I said ***Recover***
because
you can completely recover from your Alcohol Use Disorder...
you do not have to be in "perilous remission" for
the remainder of your life.

This book is not about believing that
a *power greater than yourself* could restore you to *sanity.*

While I do believe in a higher power,
I don't think that he/she/it is involved in our day-to-day lives.

Rather than requesting the assistance
of God, the Creator of the universe,
or some Power higher than you,
you will be using your *own abilities* to *rewire your brain*
to *establish new behaviors.*

You already have the power to make
any necessary changes to your lifestyle and attitude
that will free you from your unhealthy habits.

It will be the result of YOUR efforts, rather than the
intervention of a supreme being.

This book is not about you making a decision
to turn YOUR WILL and YOUR LIFE over to God.

Possibly you drank excessively to drown out or reverse
your feelings of helplessness,
which you may have found to be intolerable.

But to turn over your
FREE WILL in response to this problem
is actually the *total opposite* of what you should do...
you absolutely need to feel ***empowered***...
to be Self-Empowered.

Helplessness,
a feeling of being emotionally trapped,
can only be relieved by replacing it with *self-empowerment,*
a *sense of control* over your own life.

I do think that you need to make some changes in your life,
changes to your lifestyle, and the first one, if you have not
already done so, should be to
stop abusing alcohol, to *stop your excessive drinking.*

But that needs to be YOUR WILL because it's YOUR LIFE.

You can *believe* in God or a higher power and
still make your own choices.

Stripping you of your ability to make your own choices
is *damaging to your recovery.*

Asserting control over your own mind and will
is an act of responsibility and maturity.

Handing over your life to someone else's power is relieving you
of having to make your own decisions...
You just do what you're told...follow the rules or the steps.

Sadly, you don't even get to live your life's potential.

This book will not ask you to admit
to God, to yourself, and to another human being,
the exact *nature* of your wrongs...
your destructive behaviors...your character defects.

That is in No Way helpful to Anyone in recovery.

This book will not tell you that you need to ask God to
remove your shortcomings.
I believe that you definitely need to stop your negative behaviors
but I also think that YOU should be the one to do it.

This book is not about making a list
of all the individuals you had harmed and
making amends to them.

I expect that those who you harmed when you were
excessively drinking alcohol are aware that
it was your Alcohol Use Disorder
that greatly contributed to your negative actions
and behaviors towards them.

Of course, if you feel that it will help to ease your guilt,
then, by all means, you should apologize and
attempt to make amends.

Another way you can make amends is to continue to make
positive changes to your life,
with a firm resolve to never again engage in harmful behavior.

This book will not ask you to seek, through meditation
and prayer, to improve your conscious contact with God,
praying only for knowledge of His Will for you, and
for the power to carry it out.

Although you are certainly free to do so,
there is no place in this book where you will be encouraged

to pray to God to come to know his/her will for him/her and to
give you the means to carry it out.

Frankly, I'm not really certain what the doing of God's will
has to do with helping you recover from your Alcohol Use Disorder.

Also, in this book, you will not find any accounts of
individuals who had drinking problems,
reflecting on the awful things they experienced
while being intoxicated, horror stories of the past,
telling you, in graphic detail, just how bad things can get.

The main problem with receiving guidance and guidelines from
the dogmatic beliefs of these 12 Step programs is that
their wisdom is *outdated* and has *yet to evolve over time.*

These programs do not allow for individual questioning
or critical thinking.

Okay...
It is now time, to turn the page and find out
just what this book IS all about.

What This Book *IS* About

This Book is About...

*Self-Compassion and Self-Love

*Self-Care and Self-Improvement

*Self-Confidence, Self-Belief and Self-Empowerment

*Remaining Happily Sober, Enjoying a Healthy Sober Lifestyle.

*Finding Happiness and Contentment...
Real Happiness without HAVING to drink alcohol.

*Allowing yourself to be Happy...
because you deserve it!

*Learning about the factors that lead to
happiness and contentment and the
positive actions you can take to build a happy and content life.

*Living your life more consciously and mindfully,
with awareness.

*Feeling good about who you are and who you were
meant to be.

*Learning how to Heal and how to Recover.

*Creating a healthier lifestyle and a better life for yourself.

*Being Relentless in your pursuit of becoming your Best Self.

*Taking Responsibility for your own life rather than
pretending that it is in someone else's hands.

*Making Positive Lifetime Commitments -
To Remain Sober
To Change Your Lifestyle
To Seek Happiness and Contentment

*Reducing your Negativity and Increasing your Positivity.

*Learning how to relieve your Pain and
Unhappiness by letting go of Negative Thoughts.

*Applying Antidotes to your Destructive Negative Emotions.

*Increasing your Positive Emotions and Behaviors
by Focusing your Attention on Positive Thoughts.

*Slowing Down, Being Calm and
Feeling less Anxious and Worrisome.

*Stopping the Ruminating and the Overthinking.

*Learning to Cope with Stress...
with Life's Unavoidable Challenges and Difficulties.

*Responding to,
rather than Reacting to Life's Situations and Experiences.

*Developing Patience and Tolerance to
Help you deal more Skillfully with the Conditions or
Circumstances you may Not be Able to Change.

*Really Enjoying Life without the *need or the desire to drink alcohol.*

*Practicing Kindness and Compassion...
towards Others as well as Yourself.

*Making any necessary Changes or
Adjustments to Yourself and to Your Lifestyle.

*The Benefits of Reading and Studying
Self-Help and Self-Improvement Books.

*Training your Brain towards Happiness
through *neural plasticity.*

*The radical idea that there is a clearly
defined Path of Happiness.

*Being Grateful and Thankful for what you already have.

*Appreciating and Savoring the little,
often overlooked things in your life.

*Forgiveness — Forgiving others as well
as Forgiving yourself.

*Personal Empowerment and having
Faith, Trust and Confidence in yourself.

*Letting Go of All the Negative things in your Life.

*Letting Be or just Accepting things as they are,
whatever cannot be changed.

*Letting In all the Goodness you experience on a daily basis.

*Becoming a Better and more Complete Version of yourself.

*Realizing that NOTHING is more important than your Happiness.

*Living more In The Present Moment,
Recognizing that the Past is just held together by your Memories
and
the Future is only your Mental Image of something
that may or may not ever happen.

*The importance of practicing Self-Care Activities.

*The Power and Benefits of Meditation.

*The Importance of Mindfulness and Awareness.

*Learning how to respond to Cravings.

*Letting Go of what is Standing in Your Way of Being Happy.

*Changing your Reality by Reconditioning Yourself.

*Cultivating Love, Happiness and Contentment while reducing Fear and Unhealthy Desires.

*The Benefits of Positive Affirmations and Positive Thinking.

*Knowing the importance of having Support in Early Sobriety.

*Learning how to Forgive Yourself as well as Others.

*Enhancing, Increasing and Benefitting from your Positive Qualities or Good Character Traits.

*Learning the benefits of doing a Loving-Kindness Meditation.

*Practicing Kindness and Generosity - Giving to others as well as yourself.

*Becoming more Patient and Tolerant.

*Learning Resilience and the ability to Cope with life's problems and challenges.

*Coming to know that the Life in front of you is way more important than the Life behind you.

*Recovering - Becoming Fully Recovered.

*__Living a happy, joyful and content life, without the need or desire to drink alcohol.__

CHAPTER 5

Awareness

"The process of behavior change always
starts with awareness. You need to be
aware of your habits before you can
change them."
— James Clear

Awareness is the state of perceiving, feeling or being conscious of events, objects, or sensory patterns.

To be aware means to have knowledge or perception of a fact or a situation.

The content and quality of your life depends on your level of awareness.

The first and most vital step in finding the solution to any problem is awareness...
to be aware or conscious of the *existence* of a problem.

It is an essential step in making desired *changes.*

Without awareness, there can be *no change.*

With awareness, you can say "Enough...Something needs to *change*!"

In your case,
you recognize that you have a problem with drinking alcohol
to an excess,
to the point where it's resulting in negative actions or

behaviors,
possibly to the point where your life has,
in some way, shape or form,
become disruptive and unmanageable.

You may realize that you have an Alcohol Use Disorder (AUD)
and you need to do something about it...
to make some necessary *changes* to your life...
the first one being to immediately stop your excessive drinking.

Being honest with yourself,
made you cognizant of your problem, which, in turn,
gave you the incentive to attempt to solve it.

Although excessive drinking is a problem in itself,
it is *also* your mind's attempt to try to *solve* a problem...
to give you control...
control over your feelings of helplessness or unhappiness.

But it is, of course, just a substitutional solution.

DRINKING ALONE IS WHAT YOU DO
WHEN YOU DON'T LIKE BEING YOU

Your pattern of excessive drinking was a displacement,
a substitute for a more direct behavior.

Helplessness can only be extinguished by replacing it with
it's opposite - Self-Empowerment.

Awareness is the first step in healing and
now, with awareness,
you can begin to heal and transform your life.

(Please See Chapter 10 Healing)

Becoming *aware* is about being *responsible* for your own life.

With awareness, you have taken the first step towards a happy life
by choosing not to use alcohol
to try to escape from your unhappy reality.

Now that you've put a stop to your excessive drinking,
you can begin to approach the problem of your unhappiness,
which is what a large portion of this book deals with...
adjusting your lifestyle and
helping you create a *happier* and more *content* you!

It may appear to be selfish,
but right now, you really need to focus on YOU.

Focus on Your Self because You Deserve to be Happy...
It is, in fact, your birthright!

Allow yourself to feel happy.

You have *that right*, just like everyone else does.

Your **new life** is just beginning.

You've taken your first step on the
path of happiness and your new, sober healthy lifestyle
and it will continue to get better...
I promise you that!

It will be a transformational journey...
A journey of *Happiness Without the Need For Alcohol*

What you *will need* is strength and bravery to continue and
you will need the support of a friend,
a relative, a therapist, or someone in your support group...
someone you can trust to support you on your journey.

(Please see Chapter 17 Your Support Team)

I invite you to continue on the path of recovery...
the path of sobriety...
the path of change for the better...
the path of an wonderful new lifestyle...
the path of true happiness and contentment.

You *will need* courage to continue and
courage to *completely recover.*

Yes, Indeed, you can completely recover!

I did...
I recovered...
I really wanted to get better,
to do better, to be better...
to become happier and enjoy an alcohol-free lifestyle.

It can be done, but...
you will need courage and bravery to combat your feelings of
doubt and fear that will try to accompany you on your path.

"You will never do anything in this world
without courage. It is the greatest quality
of the mind, next to honor."
— Aristotle

Courage is critical because it is the willingness to act
in spite of being afraid.

Why we Drink Alcohol to an Excess

"People are not addicted to alcohol...they are addicted to
escaping reality."
— Unknown

Unhappiness is the feeling of not being satisfied or pleased
with a situation...
a feeling of sadness, discontent or sorrow.

We live in a culture that promotes the pursuit of
instantaneous gratification or pleasure...
the avoidance of any pain or dissatisfaction.

Some people respond to these feelings of pain by suppressing
them...
numbing themselves to their discomfort by drinking alcohol...
erroneously thinking that the effects of alcohol will
reverse their suffering.

Our culture appeals to the wanting mind, which perpetuates
the myth that happiness is contingent upon fulfilling your desires.

In search of refuge from their distress, they try to
distance themselves from pain by drowning it out with
the temporary sensory pleasure that alcohol produces.

They may feel so defeated that they seek no form of
real satisfaction, but only distraction...
becoming lovers of *pleasure...*
seeking to make life bearable by becoming less alive.

The artificial happiness that excessive drinking brings is
merely a temporary pleasure,
a diversion,
a momentary cessation of unhappiness.

Over consumption of alcohol is a symptom of your discomfort...
an indication that something in your life is being avoided...
something is out of whack, causing you pain or stressing you out...
causing you unhappiness.

There are number of reasons why people drink alcohol,
but most individuals use alcohol for one or more of the following:

...To Relax
...To Feel Confident
...To Feel Happy
...To Reduce Stress
...To Avoid Discomfort
...To Not Feel Hopeless
...To Avoid the Feeling of Not Being
Funny, Personable or Good Enough
...To Mask the Pain of Losing
Someone or Something
...To Help Cope with a Traumatic Experience

If you were to take a close look at all of these reasons,
you will see that *the foundational motivating factor* behind each
and every one of them is FEAR...
the FEAR of coming face-to-face with
your own negative thoughts, feelings and emotions.

The foundation of most of our negative thoughts and emotions
is *fear itself.*

Fear is a natural yet unpleasant emotion, that is usually
in response to perceiving or recognizing a danger or threat...
a belief that someone or something is dangerous and likely to
cause you pain.

Fear is directly connected to your *unhappiness* and so,
regardless of your specific reason or reasons for drinking alcohol
to an excess, it was ultimately
your way of temporarily avoiding *fear* or *unhappiness.*

And that is why this book is *not* just about encouraging you
to remain sober
but also to help you *reduce* your *fears* and *anxieties...*
to help you on the path to discover
real happiness and contentment.

There is absolutely nothing wrong with
making happiness your priority...
It is your birthright...
It benefits you and others as well.

"Whoever is happy, will make others
happy."
— Anne Frank

Just A Few Reasons Why I Don't Drink Anymore

I feel better, physically and emotionally, than I ever have.

I am truly enjoying life, now.

I no longer fall for the lies that alcohol promises.

I love experiencing life with 20/20 vision.

I like and respect myself more.

I don't need to wait until "happy hour" to be happy.

It is my wish that you as well, continue to progress on your
transformational journey...
on your path of happiness and contentment,
without the need or desire for alcohol.

Your Three Commitments...
1 Remain Sober
2 Change your Lifestyle
3 Seek Happiness and Contentment

If you commit to remaining sober by
JUST SAYING NO to alcohol, there is a *possibility*,
albeit a small one, that in the long run, you will succeed.

However, if you make a **commitment** to change your lifestyle
and seek happiness and contentment
as well as remain sober,
your degree of success will dramatically increase.

So, the question I have for you is this:

Are you now ready and willing to make a **commitment?**
not just a wish or a hope...
not just a decision...

Making a decision is a start but making a **commitment** goes
far beyond that.

A **commitment** involves attentiveness, dedication and
devotion, determination and effort.

It's about making a *pact* with yourself...
making it a non-negotiable priority.

Once you **commit**, you become personally responsible for your success, for your own freedom.

That really is quite empowering and right now,
that is exactly what you need...to be self-empowered.

Instead of turning over your will to some “higher power”,
you are empowering yourself...you are *strengthening your will.*

To *remain* **committed** you need to be
adaptable, patient, focused and most of all, determined.

No thing,
No person,
No place and
No situation can *make you drink...*
You choose to drink and that is why
Only You can *commit to not drink alcohol.*

There is no one that can make you
happy and content other than yourself and
there is no one who can take that away from you either.

You have to be your *biggest believer* and
strongest supporter.

Once again, your Threefold **Commitment** consists of:

1. Remaining Sober
2. Changing Your Lifestyle
3. Pursuing Happiness and Contentment

These three **commitments** share a collectively beneficial relationship...

By abstaining from alcohol and
adjusting your lifestyle,
you will become happier and more
content...

As your happiness increases,
you will find it easier to make
improvements to your lifestyle and
the positivity of your new lifestyle will
drive out any thoughts about drinking,
thereby helping you to remain sober.

It is a positive upward spiral with only beneficial effects.

You are **committing** to fundamentally *change the way* you *live.*

Know that all this is not an overnight fix...
It is not an instant solution to your difficulties...
It is a path of transformation...
a process that requires your commitment.

It will take determination, patience and
a sustained effort to establish new habits that will bring about
real happiness...
a state of happiness that will remain, despite having to deal
with life's inevitable difficulties and challenges.

You are remaining sober
so that you can find real happiness and contentment,
instead of experiencing a series of temporary,
momentary pleasures.

You have the ability, but
do you have the *willingness* to take on such a
radical change of lifestyle?

I strongly urge you to do everything in your power
to achieve and maintain your happiness.

It is worth it! You are worth it!

It's going to be life changing... in a good way.

I urge you to make that **commitment...**Make it right now!

“I choose the rest of my life to be the best of my life.”
— Louise Hay

By choosing a sober lifestyle, you will be in the minority...
but that minority is actually growing,
as people are starting to realize that
excessively drinking alcohol
is nothing more than a slow suicide.

Responsibility and Self-Empowerment

"Take charge of your own life.
Take charge of everything which is related to you.
It is you...and only you can change your own destiny."
— Amit Rao

RESPONSIBILITY

Responsibility is the opportunity or ability to act independently and make decisions without authorization.

It is accepting the fact that *you* are the *cause* and the *solution* of the matter.

It's about taking care of your own matters and answering for your own actions... being accountable for the choices you make.

Only *you* are responsible for the *quality* of your life.

SELF-EMPOWERMENT

"You feel positive about yourself to the exact degree to which you feel you are in control of your life."
— Brian Tracy

Self-Empowerment means
Taking Control of your own life...
Setting Goals
and
Making Positive Choices...
Making a Conscious Decision to Take Charge of your Destiny.

It's about having self-confidence
(a feeling of trust in your abilities, qualities and judgment)
and then taking that to the next level,
by converting your intentions into actions.

When you're self-empowered, you can
control many of the things that determine
the quality of your life.

You can exploit your strengths
as well as cope with your weaknesses.

Although the focus is on empowering yourself,
it is in no way narcissistic...
it's about taking control of *your* life,
not other people's lives.

Taking personal responsibility is both freeing and empowering
because *you decide* how to react to circumstances and situations...
but it's also about having to deal with
the consequences of your actions.

So... *Are you up for the task?*

Everything in your life, right now,
is actually a reflection of all the choices that you have ever made.

If now, you want a different result,
then you need to make different choices.

YOU are responsible for your Words,
your Behaviors, your Life.

YOU, and you alone,
have the *authority* to make decisions regarding your life.

At the same time, only YOU bear the responsibility
for the outcome of those decisions.

YOU are the final authority...
not God, not the government,
not your parents, not your spouse,
You...Only You.

But this is in no way a burden...
It is a freedom that you have.

You have the *authority,*
the *responsibility,*
the *power* and the *freedom*
to direct your life.

You do not need anyone's approval...
you just need the strength of your convictions and
faithfulness to your *Commitments!*

Feel *empowered* by your sobriety...
It's yours...
You get to *direct* it... Own it!

The degree of responsibility for your life determines
how much change you can create in it.

The more you take responsibility for,
the more you are able to create the life you seek.

You alone are responsible for the *quality* of your life...
for giving yourself the kind of life
that you want...
Make it a good one...the best you possibly can.

It is *you* who will get *you* where you want to go...no one else.

Only *you* can change *you.*

Ultimately, *you* are responsible for yourself.

Accepting responsibility empowers you
to create your own happiness...
that is the freedom that you now have...
the freedom to direct your own life.

You need to take responsibility for your own happiness.

Choose it and be responsible for it.

It's really all up to you.

You are the only one who has sole custody of your life...
your own unique life...
your entire life.

You have no need to rely on a
"higher power"...
you already have the power...
you just need to redirect it to your self...
with self-acceptance, self-compassion and self-confidence...
to your happier and more joyful life!

Self-confidence is not arrogance...
it is having a positive feeling about your ability
to live a healthy and happy sober life.

You don't have to *turn over* your power...you just have to *turn it on.*

You are your own refuge...
your own sanctuary...
your own salvation...
your own light at the end of the tunnel.

Your life is *absolutely* yours.

You alone are responsible for your actions...
you control your life by *making choices.*

It's up to you to make the choices that can create the experiences
that will bring you joy and satisfaction,
happiness and contentment...
without the need to drink alcohol.

It will take effort and energy on your behalf but
you will, without a doubt, see a positive transformation in yourself.

You will gradually let go of your unhealthy
negative emotions, beliefs and behaviors.

And, at the same time,
you will take on more positive thoughts
and emotions and increase your positive qualities.

(Please see Chapter 16 Your Positive Qualities)

You will not *just survive* but you will become
a *better version* of YOU...
a You that you will love,
with a life that you will love...
a life of joy, contentment and peace of mind.

You are in control...
You can influence your life from *this day forward,*
in a meaningful way.

If you take control of your life and
accept the responsibility for it,
by focusing on the positive and letting go of the negative,
you will realize your happiness...
not just temporary acts of momentary pleasure but
real happiness and contentment.

Maintaining control over your mind and your actions
is an act of responsibility.

You actually have the power, right now,
to create for yourself,
a better and more positive life than ever before.

The potential to make it come true lies within you.

It is a reality waiting to happen.

Bear in mind that a change will rarely occur without a
new set of conditions.

But who better than *you* to make that change...
to create the conditions necessary for the life that you envision?

Your new and happy sober life awaits you.

You can fully recover... but only you can make that happen!

My Decision to Choose a Sober Lifestyle

Hi, I'm Joey and I AM NOT an alcoholic!

I WAS addicted to alcohol but I'm not anymore.

Alcohol holds no power over me.

I HAD an Alcohol Use Disorder (AUD) but I don't anymore.

Now, I am a person who *chooses* not to drink.

I also choose not to smoke cigarettes and
I choose not to do illegal drugs.

I am a non-drinker... the same as a non-smoker.

Why???

Besides the fact that
they are all toxic
and harmful to my body and brain,
they get in the way of enjoying the many wonderful things
that life has to offer...
which I can now enjoy to the fullest,
with all my senses and 100% of my awareness.

So I CHOOSE not to drink!

Alcohol can control you and I don't like being controlled.

I like being in control of my life and
the way I choose to live it.

At first, alcohol is your friend, your pal who you can always depend on.

It tells you:
"Everything's better now"... "I've got your back"...
"I'm here whenever you need me"... "Just go and have some fun."

But inevitably it dominates your life
and
you become alcohol's bitch.

It turns against you and even steals from you...
it robs you of your most precious commodity,
Your Time.

But when you're sober, all your time is yours.

Now that I have decided not to drink alcohol,
does that mean people should believe
that I have a *problem* with alcohol?

1) What people think of me is none of my business...
   I could not care less!

2) I don't HAVE a problem with alcohol...
   I HAD a problem with alcohol... *I don't anymore!*

It requires courage to take control of your life
and be responsible for it
and it also takes a measure of self-confidence.

You may have used alcohol as a coping mechanism for a personal situation and it can be used as a coping mechanism...
It's just not a very good one.

Alcohol helps "take the edge off" or dulls your senses...
It temporarily helps you forget your problems...
It does absolutely *nothing* to help solve them.

Fortunately, now *I don't need alcohol* to help me navigate through and manage my life.

I would really rather experience life with greater clarity.

Alcohol doesn't make you happy...
It can give you a sense of euphoria...
but that is not real happiness..

I now know that I don't *need* to drink alcohol...
No one needs to drink alcohol.

Choosing not to drink alcohol is not about 'willpower' or 'discipline'...
it's not about 'deprivation'.

It's about making a conscious decision,
a COMMITMENT to not ingest something that is toxic,
both to your body and your mind.

You don't *need* alcohol to have fun.

You don't *need* alcohol to have a good time.

You don't *need* alcohol to enhance your life.

When you stop drinking alcohol,
it doesn't mean that you HAVE a problem...
It means that you HAD a problem.

You should not have to explain to anyone
why you *choose* not to drink alcohol...unless, of course, you want to.

Alcohol is a toxic, harmful, addictive chemical.

Do you have to explain to anyone why you don't smoke cigarettes
or why you don't use crack or opiates?

There is nothing embarrassing about your decision to
not consume a mind-numbing, unhealthy substance.

You have decided to quit drinking...
for whatever reason and that is no one else's business.

I don't believe that there is *anyone* who ever regretted
the day they stopped drinking.

There will be times when you need something
to help you cope with a difficult situation.

Your choice should never be alcohol...
it's *not an option.*

As I said before...it is not a healthy coping mechanism.

(Please See Chapter 32 Resilience)

Instead of viewing sobriety as a consequence...
see it as a choice...
an opportunity.

When I stopped drinking alcohol, I only achieved a part of my goal.

My complete goal was to lead a healthy and happy lifestyle
without the need or desire to drink alcohol.

I didn't want to become an unhappy, sober person.

My focus was on building or creating a happier or better life
for myself and
if I had not accomplished that,
I probably would have returned to drinking.

Today, I can confidently say that I have achieved my goal...

I have **recovered**...
I am **happy** and **content...**
I have **no desire** to drink alcohol.

When I look back on my life, I see pain, loneliness and helplessness.

Now, when I look in the mirror...
I see strength and pride in myself.

I am in competition with no one...
I have no desire to be better than anyone...
I just want to be better than the person I was yesterday.

There are *two ways* you can view your sobriety...

One is ... "I can never drink alcohol again".

The Other is... "I don't ever HAVE TO drink alcohol again".

One leads to a feeling of *deprivation...*
the other promotes a feeling of *relief.*

Our society would have you believe that alcohol is a *magic elixir...*

You drink it when there is a reason to celebrate something,
as if it will somehow enhance your feelings of happiness.

Alcohol doesn't make you happy...
it just makes you silly and most times foolish.

You take a drink when you are in a difficult situation,
believing that the effects of alcohol
will somehow provide you with the answer to your problem.

But does it ever?

You drink at the end of a long, hard day
to help you *unwind* or
reward yourself with a state of relaxation.

There are many other ways to relax
other than with a toxic substance.

Drinking alcohol *does not enhance* your life...
It Just Gets In The Way!!!

No one *needs* to have alcohol in their lives...
If they really need to drink alcohol to enjoy life,
then *that's not really living.*

By choosing not to drink,
you are going "against the grain"
and that is not a sign of weakness...
it is a sign of courage.

Sobriety alone, is not going to bring you happiness...
but it is definitely a good start!

Healing… Four Things Necessary to Begin Healing

"The natural *healing* force in each one of
us is the greatest force in getting well."
— Hippocrates

Healing is the process of making or becoming sound or healthy again.

It's about mending a wound.

In order to heal, you must stay away from what broke you…
That Is Not Optional.

To truly heal is to make whole,
which involves so much more than just
remaining sober.

To begin the process of healing in recovery, there are four things that are essential for you to do…

1. **Be Honest with Yourself**
2. **Forgive Yourself**
3. **Have Self-Compassion**
4. **Start Living in the Present**

HONESTY

"Integrity is telling myself the truth.
And honesty is telling the truth to other people."
— Spencer Johnson

Lying was something I did quite often when I had an AUD...
but I left that all behind with the alcohol abuse.

In my new sober lifestyle, I no longer have a need to be dishonest.

It's a wonderful feeling to be honest and authentic and not have to worry about being caught in a lie.

Without being honest to myself, I don't believe I would have been able to progress...
I would not have been able to start the healing process.

The path to self-healing begins with honesty...
It's about being authentic and having integrity.

To be honest means to be free of deceit and untruthfulness...
to be sincere, straightforward and genuine.

When you are honest with yourself, you
can accept all your flaws and all your weaknesses.

It is the first step to self-improvement.

Self-honesty is also necessary for you to recognize all your
inner strengths, your positive qualities, your good character traits,
which will greatly help in your healing.

(Please see Chapter 16 Your Positive Qualities)

FORGIVENESS...
Forgiving Yourself

"Forgive yourself first. Release the need to replay a negative
situation over and over again in your mind.
Do not become a hostage to your past by always reviewing and
reliving your mistakes. Do not remind yourself of what
you should have, could have or would have been.
Release it and let it go. Move on.
— Les Brown

Forgive yourself for all the bad decisions you've made...
for all the times you lacked understanding...
for all your impulsive reactions and behaviors...
for all the choices you made that caused
harm to others and to yourself...
for displaying a lack of emotional maturity...
for ALL the mistakes you made.

You made decisions based on the information you had at the time...
You have new information now and you can choose to make
more informed and positive choices.

Only by forgiving yourself, can you release all the negativity that
resides in your mind but in reality, belongs to the past...

Release it and Let it Go!

Enough of the "Should of, Would of, Could of"...
It's Time to Move On!

Do not allow your *past* to control your *present.*

You will be learning and evolving for the rest of your life,
so *stop being so hard on yourself.*

Only after you forgive yourself
can your self-rejection come to an end.

Once your self-acceptance begins, your self-love will begin to grow.

Forgive Yourself!
Accept Yourself!
Encourage Yourself!
Love Yourself!

All are necessary to welcome in the life you want...
the life you deserve.

SELF-COMPASSION

"If your compassion does not include yourself, it is incomplete."
— Buddha

Compassion starts with understanding that everyone you meet
is fighting their own battles, of which you know nothing.

To have compassion is to have concern for the sufferings or
misfortunes of others...
It literally means "to suffer with".

It is more than just having empathy...
It is to feel deeply for another person as they experience the ups
and downs associated with life...
It is a feeling of motivation to relieve the suffering in others.

You feel a warmth, a caring and a desire to help
alleviate the suffering of an other.

Having compassion towards someone, means that you would offer
understanding and kindness when they make mistakes or
undergo failures.

And Self-Compassion?

That's just offering that same kindness and understanding
to *yourself,*
whenever *you* are suffering or
hurting in some way, as you would anyone else.

Self-Compassion is a form of *acceptance...*
an acceptance of yourself
when you are feeling hurt or pain.

It is also a form of *kindness...*
giving yourself the same kindness that you would give
to someone else that is suffering.

Self-compassion is natural...
it is just focusing on your desire to be safe...
It is recognizing that **you** are deserving of happiness.

Self-Compassion is about having warmth and understanding
towards yourself
when you feel inadequate or feel like a failure.

STOP with the SELF-CRITICISM

Do not let your Inner Critic tell you how you should
or should not feel...
that only increases your suffering.

Instead, offer kindness, understanding and compassion to yourself
as you would to someone you love, who is hurting and in pain.

Treat yourself with decency, dignity and respect,
because you deserve it.

Be sensitive and considerate of your own needs.

Have love and understanding for yourself.

Care about yourself...wish yourself happiness instead of sadness.

Be on your own side...
not against anyone, but for yourself.

As a person in recovery, you need to be your own best friend...
someone you value...

someone you care for...
someone you enjoy being with...
someone you appreciate, even with
all your mistakes and flaws...
someone you would do anything for.

Pain is a part of life...it is unavoidable...
Self-Compassion is about comforting yourself
in the midst of your pain.

Some affirmations you could use to help promote self-compassion:

(See Chapter 14 Positive Affirmations)

I love and accept myself, unconditionally!

Everyday, I am doing the best I can!

I am worthy of being happy!

It's okay to make mistakes...it doesn't mean that I'm a failure!

I am becoming a better version of myself, everyday!

I am calm and in control of how I feel!

I give myself the gift of unconditional love!

I am a positive being, aware of my potential!

I choose to be happy and completely love myself!

I am in control of my thoughts and my life!

Practice a Loving-Kindness Meditation (Chapter 35)
or a mantra using the following phrases:

May I be truly happy

May I live in peace

May I live in love

May I know the power of forgiveness

May I recognize that my life has purpose

Having compassion for yourself also paves the way for you
to build up your resilience...
which is vital for coping with life's challenges, especially in recovery.

LIVING IN THE PRESENT

"We do not *heal* the past by dwelling
there. We heal the past by *living fully* in
the present."
— Marianne Williamson

You need to come to terms with the fact that
you cannot change the past...
You can learn from it, but you can never change it.

You cannot change what you did in the past but
you can change yourself for the better,
right now,
in the present,
and then move forward.

It is *always* the present...
It is *always* now...
It is *where life resides.*

If your mind is in the past, you cannot be here, in the present.

What's done is done... forgive yourself...Get Over It!

(Please See Chapter 24 Living in the Present Moment)

Managing Stress in Sobriety

Now that you are a non-drinker,
how will you deal with the everyday stresses and challenges
that are part of life?

Obviously, alcohol is not an option...
Besides, you already know that it is not a good coping mechanism.

There are, however, other effective ways to deal with stress.

The key is...
finding out how to *manage* and *relieve* stress in *healthy* and *positive* ways.

The following practices are essential to your recovery as well as your happiness.

SELF-CARE

To compete in any event requires being in shape and
one of the best ways to become in shape, in order to handle
the stresses and challenges that life will throw your way,
especially in your recovery
is by practicing **self-care**.

Self-Care is the practice of activities that
you initiate and perform on your behalf in maintaining your life,
your health and your well-being.

It helps to create a positive, more confident you...
a you, who can take on life's challenges.

(For a list of self-care strategies, Please Go To Chapter 13 Self-Care)

DAILY SCHEDULE

One thing that was essential for me, in my early sobriety was to
create a **daily schedule.**

Having a reasonable schedule will help eliminate too much free time,
resulting in boredom.

Boredom can be a catalyst for relapse... AKA a trigger.

On the other hand, a poorly planned, jam packed schedule
with no time to relax and recharge,
will only add unnecessary stress.

The key is to create a well balanced daily plan,
that includes time for self-care.

EXERCISE

A big part of self-care involves exercise.

One of the most important parts of my daily routine was,
and still is, **exercise.**

Exercise may just be the *ultimate calming technique.*

It lowers your cortisol levels, which can
become dangerously high when you're under too much stress...
releases endorphins, which are natural painkillers and mood boosters...
improves the quality of your sleep...
boosts your confidence and self-worth,

leaving you in a more prepared position
to manage and reduce stress.

(For more on the benefits of Exercise Please See Chapter 37)

NATURE

Another way to help manage stress is by spending time in **nature.**

Whether you take a walk in a park, by a river, a lake, or the ocean...
go hiking in the woods or just spend time in your garden...
or even with your indoor plants and flowers,
you will receive the healing properties of nature on your well-being...
bringing both your body and mind into balance.

Having a balanced, calm and peaceful mind will help keep you
in a more effectual position to handle life's problems.

(For more on the positive effects of Nature, Please See Chapter 38)

LEARNING

One of the reasons I wanted to write this book was to share
all that I learned
from my daily **reading** and **studying** of
self-help and self-improvement books.

They have helped and continue to help me interpret myself and
my world with more positivity.

Learning, with self-improvement books can serve as a tool to help
fight against life's challenges.

(For more on the benefits of Self-Help and Self-Improvement books,
Please See Chapter 36)

POSITIVE THINKING AND AFFIRMATIONS

Also critical in early sobriety is
positive thinking.

Nothing happening in your life will cause you to have stress...
Stress occurs from *your thoughts* about your life.

There are a number of ways
to direct your mind toward positive thoughts.

I believe that positive affirmations
are the most direct and maybe the most effective way.

Here are some
Positive Affirmations for Early Sobriety that I found helpful:

I deserve great things and I am worthy of great things!

I forgive myself for the things I did while under the influence of alcohol!

My strength is stronger than the temptation of alcohol!

I am in control of my life!

I am making progress every day!

I can do this and I will do this!

The past does not control me now!

I am strong!

I am becoming the person I want to be!

I control the narrative of my life!

To be effective, affirmations require *repetition*.

Choose one or more of these affirmations and say them out loud
as many times throughout your day, as you can
and if you can,
as soon as you wake up each day and before you go to sleep at night.

Focusing on *positive thoughts* will lead to positive emotions...
which will leave less room for harmful, negative thoughts,
which are the actual source of your stress.

By making an effort to regularly think positive thoughts,
you will *counteract* your brain's "negativity bias" or
tendency to focus on the negative.

Through regular repetition of positive affirmations and
consciously focusing on the positive,
your brain will create new neural pathways leading to more
positive thinking patterns and beliefs.

Your new positivity will serve as a safeguard against any stress
you may experience in your sobriety,
in your recovery,
in your life.

(For a full list of affirmations, See Chapter 14 Positive Affirmations)

MEDITATION

Stress can cause you to become anxious, tense and worried.

Practicing **meditation** can restore your calm and inner peace and
help reduce your stresses.

Mindfulness meditation is about being mindful,
having an increased awareness and acceptance of living in
the present moment.

It's about focusing on the flow of your breath,
observing your thoughts and emotions,
letting them pass without judgment.

(See Chapter 15 Meditation, to learn a basic meditation practice)

EXPRESSING GRATITUDE

Gratitude is about being thankful and appreciative of everything in your life.

Having gratitude can help protect you from life's challenges and problems.

An appreciation of your current circumstances will help you
to cope by reinterpreting your stressful challenges in a positive way.

You will always have disappointments and misfortunes and these can be a challenge to your sobriety.

By practicing gratitude...
being thankful and focusing your attention on the good in your life,
you will help create positive thoughts and feelings,
leaving you fortified to take on life's stresses.

(To learn more about being grateful, See Chapter 33 Gratitude)

These are some of the strategies that
will help you to manage stress, especially in early sobriety.

As I only touched on some of the benefits,
I sincerely hope that you flip over to the suggested chapters
to gain more insight from these stress reducing strategies.

And lastly…

"Always remember,
you are braver than you believe,
stronger than you seem,
smarter than you think and
twice as beautiful as you ever imagined."
— Doctor Seuss

Cravings

A craving is an intense or powerful desire...
a hunger, a longing, a yearning or an urge for something.

Do not be afraid of having a craving...
it is perfectly natural.

Cravings do not mean that you are still addicted,
that alcohol holds any power over you or
that you will always be someone with an Alcohol Use Disorder.

I have not smoked a cigarette in decades and yet, once in a while,
I still get a craving to smoke.

Cravings are mostly mental...and that's a good thing.

A craving begins as a thought...
only a thought and
thoughts, in and of themselves,
hold no power over you.

If, however, you attend to this thought and engage with it,
it can trigger an emotion...
which may prompt you to act upon it.

But a thought is just in your head...
and a thought can always be changed.

It Is Not the Boss of You!

You can dismiss it, argue with it, laugh at it, or just ignore it.

That might work...But what if it returns?

Although a craving starts out as a thought,
it does have the potential to intensify and try to control you...
but *only* if you allow it to develop into a feeling or an emotion.

If you do allow it to control you,
that emotion may unreasonably try to convince you to pick up a drink.

Obviously then, you need to have a *strategy...*
a stronger defense.

Fortunately there are a number of tactics that you can use
to conquer or defeat your craving:

1 Bring to mind the
harmful consequences of what usually happens when you drink...
reminding you of why you stopped drinking in the first place
and why you are choosing to live a life without alcohol and
why you should deny that craving.

2 Replace that negative thought with a positive one...
focus on some of the wonderful things that
living life without alcohol, has to offer.

3 Remind yourself of your three commitments:

To remain Sober
To change your Lifestyle
To seek Happiness and Contentment

Are you really going to ignore your resolutions?...
just give up and allow yourself to be defeated by a craving?
by nothing more than a thought in your head?

Have respect for your commitments!

4 Do something physical...take a walk or a hike, exercise, put on some music, dance, sing, play a musical instrument.

As soon as you start moving, the thoughts in your head begin to quiet down.

5 Reach out to someone in your support system - a friend, a family member, someone in your support group.

You have a number of options or choices in how you can successfully respond.

One of these strategies will work to defeat your craving.

Cravings may continue to come back from time to time, but each time you defeat them, they will lose more of their power.

The next time you get a craving,
try not to fight it...
that will just make it worse.

Use whichever strategy, or combination thereof, that works best for you.

Stay calm and relax in the knowledge that
it will eventually pass.

However, if you *do* experience a relapse, *do not feel defeated.*

Instead of beating yourself up, show kindness to yourself, forgive yourself and start again.

Life is all about second chances.

Remind yourself that you deserve to be happy...**YOU REALLY DO!**

CHAPTER 13

Self-Care

"Self-care is a deliberate choice to gift
yourself with people, places, things,
events and opportunities that recharge
your personal battery and promote
whole health - body, mind and spirit."
— Laurie Buchanan

It's kinda like that!

Self-Care is the practice of taking action to preserve or
improve one's own health.

It is the practice of taking an active role in
protecting one's well-being and happiness.

Self-care is making a conscious effort to
care for your own physical, mental and emotional health...
taking care of yourself
by engaging in strategies that promote
healthy functioning and enhance your well-being.

But Self-Care is not just about eating and sleeping well and
drinking plenty of water...

It's also about giving yourself a break when you need one...
saying 'No' to things you really don't want to do...
allowing yourself to be vulnerable and cry when you need to...
asking for help when you can't do something alone...
doing what really makes you happy.

You've recently stopped your excessive drinking...
Your mind and body are going through changes...
possibly some challenging adjustments.

At this time of healing and recovery,
you might want to be *extra kind* to yourself...
have some compassion for yourself.

(Please see the section on Self-Compassion in Chapter 10 Healing)

It's also vital for you to build up your resilience,
so you can handle the stresses and challenges
that life will continue to throw at you.

Taking care of yourself is not about "*You First*"...
It's about "*You Also*".

Self-care is not selfish or narcissistic...
it's not a luxury,
and it's not just about pampering yourself.

It is essential to equip yourself to be in position to
live your new healthy, happy,
sober lifestyle.

It's not a one-size-fits-all strategy.

Some self-care practices you can do occasionally,
others, you might want to do every day and yet
others you may not find the need to do at all...

It's entirely up to you...
I'm just throwing out some suggestions.

Here are some examples of self-care you may want to engage in...
do a couple, do a few, do some or do them all...

Listen to or Dance to the Music that you love...
Rock, Blues, Jazz, Country, Classical, Hip Hop, Metal,
R&B, Rap, Bluegrass, Reggae or whatever...
because music is the strongest form of magic.

Drink more Water...
Tap water, Bottled water, Sparkling water, Flavored water...
And don't wait until you're thirsty.

Drinking water is like taking a shower for your insides...
your liver, especially, will thank you.

Enough with the "fast food" already...
Eat more Healthy Foods...
You owe it to yourself.
It's not only good for your body but for your mind as well,
because when you make your body happy,
it lets your mind know about it.

Wake Up Early, *on purpose...*
you'll have added time to exercise, which helps lower your
stress levels...
it will increase your focus...
improve your sleep patterns
and it just makes you feel good all day long.

Exercise...
aerobic, anaerobic or both...
just get your body moving...the benefits are endless.

Walk...fast or slow, whenever you can, as far as you can,
for as long as you can and as often as you can...
Once again, just get your body moving.

(Please See Chapter 37 The Benefits of Exercise)

Spend time in Nature...
take in its beauty with all your senses...
Hike the trails...
Do this for at least two or three hours a week.

(Please see Chapter 38 Nature and Hiking in Nature)

Sleep Well...
try for a straight seven or eight hours...
Better Sleep = Better Mood = Happier You

Meditate...
Try to make this a daily practice...
It doesn't have to be a formal meditation...
you can do it almost anywhere and at any time.

(Please See Chapter 15 Meditation)

Read...
whatever makes you feel good...
Fictional books provide a respite from life's stresses...
Non-fictional, self-help and self-improvement books can be invaluable.

(Please see Chapter 36 My Self-Improvement Journey)

Play or learn to play an instrument...
This is one of the best forms of therapy...
a proven way to help reduce stress.

Watch or Listen to Comedy...
Stand-up, Seinfeld reruns, Road Runner or Bugs Bunny cartoons...
whatever gets you laughing.
Laughter releases endorphins (the body's natural feel-good chemicals).

Do something novel or new,
something that you've never done before,
something you've always wanted to do.

Write...
about how you feel, even if it's just a word or two, every day...
about what you're grateful for...
about positive things that you like.
I'm doing it right now and whether or not anyone reads this,
it still helps me feel good.

Take a break from social media...
It's leaves you more time for some necessary emotional
well-being practices...
It allows you to live more "in the present moment".

(Please See Chapter 24 Living in the Present)

Connect with Friends or Family...
preferably in person or, at the very least, by phone or text.

Spend Time with your furry friends, your dog, or your cat...
Just *be* with them...
Let them help you to slow down and stay present.

Practice Random Acts of Kindness...
It's a win/win... good for the person on the receiving end and
it makes you feel good as well.

(Please See Chapter 34 Kindness and Generosity)

Relax and Recharge...
Relaxation is the state of being free from tension and anxiety...
Make time for yourself, some quiet time...
Do this every day whether you think you need it or not.

Smile, whether it feels natural or not...
I put on a smile almost every morning,
especially if I wake up a bit anxious.
Your brain doesn't know if it's involuntary or not...
it still releases endorphins, which make you feel good.

(Please See Chapter 39 Smiling and Laughing)

Volunteer your Time...
There are many organizations that would appreciate your help
(another win/win).

Call someone in your support group...
if you need to talk about your sobriety or
just to see how they are doing.

Celebrate your Achievements...
It's good to feel good about your progress and
your determination to stay faithful to your commitments...
Do something special for yourself.

Never forget that you are worth investing in.

Self-care helps you to feel good, physically and emotionally, and
feeling good is the foundation of happiness and contentment.

Positive Affirmations

"What you think, you become.
What you feel, you attract.
What you imagine, you create."
— Buddha

What you *believe about yourself* becomes *your truth.*
What you tell yourself becomes *your reality.*

If your life is not exactly the way you want it,
affirmations can help
to turn your thinking and existence in a positive direction.

Affirmations are positive statements and reminders
you repeat to yourself that motivate and empower you.

These statements are powerful tools, used to promote
positive thinking
that can help change the way you see yourself and your life.

These positive statements can help you to challenge and
overcome self-sabotaging, negative thoughts.

When you repeat them often, and
really start believing them,
you will start to make positive changes.

Positive affirmations are very powerful because
they help to release you from fears, worries and anxieties.

When repeated over and over,
they begin to take charge of your thoughts...

they become *your thoughts*...
slowly changing your pattern of thinking and
ultimately changing your life.
Using affirmations can give you the thought patterns
you need to create positivity circuits.

Positive affirmations actually *reprogram*
or *retrain* your brain...to think more positively.

It's like exercise for your mind.

It is possible
through the neural plasticity of your brain...
its ability to be molded or changed.

(Please see Chapter 23 Training Your Brain)

Positive affirmations can also increase the amount of
feel-good hormones in your brain...
which are very helpful in your early sobriety.

Positive thoughts create positive emotions,
which can change your physiology and improve
your mental, emotional and physical health.

With enough repetition, positive affirmations offer a way to
modify your thinking in a positive way...
Gradually your corresponding beliefs and
behaviors will follow,
thereby shaping your existence and creating a new life.

Here are some examples of positive affirmations you might want to try:

I focus on what I *can* control and let go
of what I can't!

I choose not to drink alcohol!

I am in charge of my happiness!

My thoughts do not need to lead to actions.

I am stronger than I know!

I'm replacing my habits with new positive ones!

My life is moving in the right direction!

I am motivated and strong!

I am mindful of every action I take!

My past does not define my future!

I am growing and learning every day!

I am not missing out on anything good!

I choose to exercise my self-control!

My mindset is strong and unwavering!

I am progressing, advancing and growing!

Emotionally, I feel stable and secure!

I forgive myself for the things I did when I was abusing alcohol!

I am stronger than any craving!

The past doesn't control me anymore!

I'm becoming the person I want to be!

I control the narrative of my life!

I release the pain from my past and my anxiety about the future!

I believe in myself and my abilities!

I am feeling empowered!

I choose to be kind, to myself and others!

I am in charge of my thoughts and feelings!

I stand firm in my commitments and will not compromise!

My confidence increases every day!

I completely accept myself!

I am finding joy in all the little things!

I don't let others' judgments affect me!

I am thankful for all I have!

I'm proud of myself for staying committed!

I am calm, peaceful and safe!

I have everything I need within me!

All is well in my world!

I have the capability to overcome any of life's challenges!

I am centered, peaceful and grounded!

I have the strength to rise in the face of adversity!

I will not worry about everything!

I will live a healthy lifestyle!

I'm becoming more at ease with myself!

I will be honest with myself!

I do not need to control everything!

I will allow life to play out on its own!

I have the courage to say No!

I am fearless!

I am focused and ready for the day!

I will succeed!

I have the power to let go of the negative!

My well-being is my top priority!

I choose to be calm!

I am grateful for this day!

I choose to let go of my worries and my stress!

My sensitivity is my strength!

I will focus on the positive, today!

I am at peace even when life is crazy!

I release all tension from my body and my mind!

Choose some that feel right for you or
make some of your own.

Of course, the most important affirmation should be
the one regarding your drinking of alcohol...
which will actually evolve over time —

In Early Sobriety

An essential affirmation of yours in early sobriety should be::

I will **NOT DRINK TODAY** !!!

Repeat this everyday, for as many times as you are able to,
throughout each day..

In Recovery

In the latter part of your recovery, your affirmation should be:

I CHOOSE NOT to **DRINK** !!!

Not now, not later, not tonight, not after work, not this weekend.

After You Have Recovered

After you have recovered and yes, it is most definitely
possible to fully recover...
you will not suffer with AUD for the rest of your life
if you take the responsibility,
stay faithful to your commitments and
know that your life is so much better without alcohol...

I HAVE NO NEED to **DRINK ANYMORE** !!!

You are not an "alcoholic in recovery" for the rest of your life.

You are someone who *had* an Alcohol Use Disorder.

Now, you are just a ***non drinker...*** *By Choice.*

These positive mental repetitions,
practiced as often as you can,
will change your thinking patterns,
so that over time,
you will be motivated to think and behave in
more positive ways.

The power of positive affirmations lies in repetition...
repeat them to yourself until they make their way
into your belief system and thought processes.

(Please see Chapter 23 Training Your Brain)

Try to find some that resonate with you...
the sooner you trust them to be true,
the sooner they will have a positive effect on your thinking.

They are definitely one of the most useful and
important tools you have available to you, in your recovery.

Meditation

Meditation is a simple practice available to everyone, which can reduce your stress, increase your calmness, sharpen your clarity and promote happiness.

But meditation is *not about trying to relax.*

Meditation is
training your attention so you can be more aware of
your own inner workings
as well as
what is happening around you in the here and now.

As you learn more about yourself,
you will become less surprised by your feelings
that arise during meditation...
helping you develop a less reactive relationship
with your emotions.

Once you can see clearly what's going on in the moment,
you can choose *whether* and
how to act on what you are seeing.

Alcohol obscures the clarity and depth of your mind.

Learning to focus your attention through meditation
will bring a sense of calmness and clarity to your mind...
you will discover the depths of happiness and well-being
that no sensory pleasure can compare to.

A SIMPLE, BASIC MEDITATION

1 Find a comfortable position, either sitting or lying down.

2 Close your eyes and try to relax.

3 Take some long, deep breaths —
inhale for about four seconds, then
exhale for four...
Focus on your breathing.

4 Notice any thoughts that arise...
Do not try to resist them...
just allow them to come up and pass
without any judgment or attachment to
them.

5 When your mind wanders (and it will)
return to and focus on your breath...
this will help you to stay grounded,
connected and focused on the moment.

6 After about three to five minutes or so,
gently open your eyes.

7 Repeat steps 1 through 6 on a daily basis.

Meditation is the practice of *not getting lost in thought.*

But do not try to stop your thinking.

Be aware when thoughts arise and
notice the impermanent,
insubstantial nature of your thoughts.

Often in the moment of awareness,
your thoughts simply liberate or disappear.

Practice remaining undisturbed and distracted
as your thoughts arise.

During meditation, do not try to resist your thoughts...
just attend to the moment...stay with the breath...and allow
your thoughts to stop on their own.
Give yourself permission to have thoughts.

The more you try to control your thoughts,
the more they will gain strength.

Give your mind some space and
it will quiet down on it's own.

Try to control it, quiet or restrict it, and it will run wild.

Let your thinking stop by itself.

You cannot determine what emotions will arise,
nor can you totally control your emotions.

But through meditation,
you can *change your response to them.*

Meditation will help you to see that
everything in life is impermanent.

Meditation gives you the ability to cultivate positive emotions,
retain emotional stability and engage in mindful behavior.

The skills you learn in meditation
are transferable to the rest of your life...
You learn how to stay in the moment...
how to let go of judgments...
become aware of a calm, stable center
that can be steady even when facing life's challenges...
be kinder to yourself and
become more self-reliant.

Meditation can increase your levels of
feel-good chemicals, endorphins and serotonin,

providing feelings of calm and relaxation.
It can also help increase your happiness
and contentment and reduce any negativity.

Anchoring your attention in the breath
does more than cultivate a focused, calm mind.

It allows you to see how your mind works...
how it easily wanders, compares, judges and labels.

Knowing that, you can always take refuge in your anchor,
the breath,
which will help give you the courage to explore your mind.

Lying below the surface of your
consciousness are your inherent qualities
of *calm, well-being, kindness and love.*

Everything you need, your courage, strength, compassion
and love, is already inside you.

With continued practice, meditation can help you assess,
recognize and even
enhance those positive qualities.

The more you meditate,
the more you will become confident
in your innate goodness and positivity.

As you begin feeling these positive qualities of mind,
you will have less need to rely on any external conditions
for your happiness and contentment.

The Buddha was asked:
"What have you learned from meditation?"
He replied "Nothing...but what I have lost
is anger, anxiety, depression, insecurity and
fear of old age and death."

Your Positive Qualities

Drinking alcohol excessively to numb your pain and suffering
is like putting a bandaid on melanoma...
When the bandaid falls off, the cancer is still there!

You have been unsuccessful in using a temporary,
external substance to try and fix an internal problem.

Does that, in itself, make you a bad person?
Should your unwise attempt to soothe your feelings
of helplessness detract from or diminish any of your good qualities?

Step 4 of AA's 12 Step Program asks you to
"make a searching and fearless *moral* inventory" of yourself.

"Step 4 is our vigorous and painstaking effort to discover what
these liabilities in each of us have been, and are.
We want to find exactly how, when, and where our natural desires
have warped us. We wish to look squarely at the unhappiness
this has caused others and ourselves..."

(The Big Book - Alcoholics Anonymous by Bill W. p42&p43)

Nothing you did was immoral!

You only acted according to your *level of awareness* at that time.

You mind had been clouded with negativity, which held you back
from thinking clearly.

If you had been more conscious, more aware, more mindful,
you would have acted differently.

There is no need to feel guilty over something you did
when you were not the person who you are now.

An *action* from a *suffering person*, in the past, *does not represent*
who that person is forever.

Positive qualities are your personal attributes, good character traits
or inner strengths...
they serve as a protection to your
well-being.

Cultivating positive qualities leads to experiencing positive emotions.

I would like to ask you now to please take an inventory,
write down all of your *positive qualities...*
all of your good character traits...
your valuable inner strengths.

If you get stuck, perhaps you can ask a friend or family member
for some assistance...
I'm certain they can think of a few.

I have also listed below, some positive qualities for you to peruse.

I believe this is an important project for you,
as when you are finished, you will realize that
YOU are fundamentally, a *good person...*
with a number of good, positive qualities or
character traits..

Some of them, may however, be somewhat underdeveloped...

but with awareness, intentional practice and a bit of effort,
they can be strengthened.

No doubt as you read through the list of positive qualities
that can help lead you to happiness and contentment,
you will see some that you may still need to work on.

These traits will lead you to improving your character
and help you find true happiness.

This is one of a number of strategies you may use
to assist you in finding lasting happiness and contentment.

Some Examples of Positive Qualities:

Kind - friendly and good natured

Considerate - careful not to inconvenience or hurt anyone

Gentle - showing a mild or tender character

Caring - having concern for others

Honest - sincere and free of deceit

Loyal - showing firm support of allegiance

Appreciative - feeling or showing gratitude

Sensitive - delicate appreciation of another's feelings

Patient - ability to accept or tolerate problems
without being annoyed

Thoughtful - showing consideration for others

Trustworthy - able to be relied on as honest or truthful

Polite - having respectful behavior

Generous - giving more than what is expected

Grateful - appreciative or thankful

Fair - upright and impartial

Respectful - courteous and gracious

Forgiving - ready and willing to forgive

Conscientious - wanting to do what is right

Optimistic - hopeful and confident about the future

Courageous - not deterred by danger or pain

Humble - not thinking less of yourself but
thinking of yourself less

Compassionate - the feeling that arises when you are
confronted with another's suffering and feel motivated
to relieve that suffering.

Responsible - capable of being trusted

Trustworthy - able to be relied on as honest or truthful

Determined - having made a firm decision and
being resolved not to change it

Friendly - kind and pleasant, amiable and cordial

Open-Minded - unprejudiced, willing to consider new ideas

Wise - having or showing experience, knowledge
and good judgment

Attentive - paying close attention to someone or something

Realistic - having or showing a sensible and practical idea
of what can be achieved or expected

Helpful - giving or ready to give help

Self-Disciplined - the ability to control one's feelings and
overcome one's weaknesses...
the ability to pursue what one thinks is right
despite temptations to abandon it.

Easy Going - relaxed and tolerant in approach or manner

Reasonable - having sound judgment, fair and sensible

I'm sure there are a number of these qualities that you see in yourself.

These personal qualities can help protect you as they serve as
your inner strengths...
your protectors in combating life's challenges and difficulties.

Write down the personal strengths you plan to work on...
then, each day, be determined to put them into action.

Doing this will, without a doubt, contribute your
ultimate happiness and contentment.

Your Support Team

High on the top the list of things that can aid you in your sobriety
is having a support system.

Although the responsibility of staying true to your
commitment of remaining sober is yours,
it helps to know that you are not all alone.

As mentioned in Chapter 5 Awareness,
you will need courage to continue in your new sober lifestyle...
you will also need the support of a friend,
a family member or a therapist...
someone you can trust to support you on your journey.

There is no easy way to share your drinking problem
with your friend, your family member or even your therapist
but it is important that you do.

It's a scary thing to be vulnerable, but to share your secrets
with someone is an important part of the recovery process.

You are responsible for putting in place your
personal support team.

At the very least,
you need to confide in someone close to you,
your goals or commitments to remain sober, modify your lifestyle
and seek happiness and contentment.

Perhaps discussing this with a close friend or family member
and asking for their support is all you may need.

Support groups...
although not *absolutely* necessary, can be quite beneficial in that, participating in these groups are people who are going through or have gone through something similar to what you are experiencing.

Knowing this can encourage you to maintain your sobriety, and you, in turn, may encourage others as well.

The importance of the support of your peers in the recovery process should not be underestimated.

They can help you because those in the support group are all working towards the same goal of sustained sobriety.

It's always good to have people you can lean on, especially those who have already been where you are now.

There are some peer groups that get together in person and quite a few that meet online.

Most of these are free to join with their only requirement being your willingness to remain sober.

There are quite a number of *alternatives* to the 12 step programs...
These are just a few:

SMART Recovery
Women for Sobriety
LifeRing Secular Recovery
Moderation Management

and the one I participated in, online, in my early sobriety, Refuge Recovery, which was extremely helpful and highly recommended.

I'm sure there are dozens more you can research as more and more people are starting to realize that the 12 Step programs are not the only support groups that exist and 12 Step groups are not for everyone.

I believe that support groups can be very helpful to you,
especially in your early sobriety.

My suggestion would be to utilize them for at least
six to nine months.

After that, it's up to you...
that may be all you'll need or you may want to
continue indefinitely.

It's a personal choice...
and as with most things in your recovery,
you get to make the call because...
you alone are responsible for your sobriety,
for changing your lifestyle
and becoming happy and content.

Your Thoughts and Positive Thinking

"Don't believe every worried thought you
have. Worried thoughts are notoriously
inaccurate."
— Renee Jain

Your Thoughts

A thought is an idea, a notion, a view or
an opinion produced by thinking, or occurring suddenly
in the mind.

Do not believe all the thoughts that come into your head...
they are an endless stream of ideas running wild through
your mind.

Not all of those thoughts are totally true.

Many of the thoughts that pop into your head are
not even based on reality.

They might just be your opinions or judgments based on
unfair comparisons.

And, not all of those thoughts come from you.

They could just be words you remember hearing from someone
else, or something that you saw posted on social media,
which may or may not be true.

Some of the thoughts that pop into your head
might not be good for you.

You cannot control the thoughts that enter your brain,
but you *can choose how you will deal with them.*

You give power, only to the thoughts that you
choose to give your attention to.

They are powerless until you decide to make them *your thoughts.*

Only the thoughts you focus on or give your attention to,
will actually become *your thoughts.*

The happiness of your life depends on the quality of *your thoughts.*

Your thoughts help to create the *emotions* that you feel.

Those feelings or emotions, triggered by *your thoughts*,
reinforce your thinking, which helps shape your beliefs
and your beliefs, in turn,
form the basis for the actions you take...your behaviors and habits.

Over time, your behaviors eventually help to create your
personal qualities or character traits, good or bad.

This is how **your thoughts** help to **create your reality**...
who you really are.

Your thoughts are the *foundation* of your experiences and
therefore are responsible for the creation of your life.

"You mind is everything. What you think, you become."
— Buddha

Only by changing **your thoughts** can you change
your feelings and emotions.

Your emotions, one by one, will gradually modify
your thinking patterns or beliefs.

Changing your beliefs will have a direct effect on your actions
and behaviors, which, represent who you are.

Because your thinking patterns, your beliefs, dictate your reality...
if you want to change your reality,
you *must* change your thinking.

When you recognize the power that those thoughts
you intentionally focus on, have on your actions and behaviors,
you begin to realize that it is ***you*** who has the responsibility
for your actions and behaviors...
you are in control of your decisions...
you are in control of *your thoughts* and ultimately *your life.*

Positive Thinking

"Your mind is a powerful thing. When you
fill it with positive thoughts, your life will
start to change."
— Unknown

What do you require...what do you really need to remain sober,
have a healthy lifestyle and become a happy person?

What is necessary for you to remain faithful
to your Three Commitments?

You require no more than anyone else who desires to live
a happy and content life...

MORE POSITIVITY and LESS NEGATIVITY.

The best place to start creating more positivity in your life is
with **your thoughts**, *your thinking.*

Positive psychology stresses the importance of
cultivating **positive thinking** through
positive affirmations (Chapter 14)
meditation (Chapter 15)
mindfulness (Chapter 25)
savoring positive experiences (Chapter 28)
increasing your positive qualities or character traits(Chapter 16)...
all of which starts with your own thoughts.

Positive thinking doesn't mean avoiding or ignoring
the bad things in life...
You don't totally disregard the bad...
you just don't focus on it.

Positive thinking is about having an optimistic attitude...
approaching life's situations with the expectation
that everything will work out,
rather than contemplating the bad and anticipating chaos.

Positive thinking is a healthy mental and emotional attitude
that focuses on the bright side of life...
anticipating positive results.

It's about making the most of potentially bad situations...
trying to see the best in others...
viewing yourself and your abilities in a positive light.

To cultivate this positive thinking,
you first need to become aware of the thoughts that you focus on,
those thoughts to which you give your attention.

The choice is entirely yours.

You are responsible for choosing the thoughts you will
make part of your thinking... *your thoughts.*

Only by directing your mind toward positive thoughts
can you begin a positive upward spiral leading to
favorable emotions, optimistic beliefs,

constructive actions and behaviors and ultimately, *a more positive you.*

And creating more positivity in your life will help you to keep your *Three Commitments* of

...Remaining Sober
...Maintaining your New Lifestyle
...Continuing on your Path of Happiness and Contentment

"It isn't what you have or who you are or where you are or what you are doing that makes you happy or unhappy. It is what you think about."
— Dale Carnegie

Negative Thoughts...how to let them go

"Positive people have negative thoughts...
They just don't let those thoughts
control them."
— Unknown

Today, we live in a society that is focused more on the negative
than the positive.

Add to that, the fact that we all have inherited a *negativity bias,*
and it's no wonder that we continue to have an abundance of
negative thoughts streaming through our minds.

This 'negativity bias' is the tendency to register negative stimuli
more readily than the positive.

This "positive-negative asymmetry",
as it is sometimes referred to,
is our tendency to recall reprimands far more often than praise.

It is likely that we inherited this 'negativity bias' through evolution,
from our ancestors.

For them, paying attention to dangerous and negative threats
was a matter of life and death...
Constantly anticipating an attack was critical to their survival.

Those who paid attention to potential threats were
those who were likely to survive and pass on this "negativity bias"
to future generations.

This is why first impressions affect us so strongly...
why we are likely to notice
negative occurrences more than positive ones and
then remember the negative ones more vividly in the future.

We all have a tendency to —

React more strongly to negative stimuli

Recall insults sooner than praise

Remember traumatic experiences better
than we do positive ones

Think about negative things much more
frequently than positive ones

Keep in mind that
the thoughts you have are not always based on facts...
and since those thoughts may be built on non-factual thinking,
they're really just based on feelings or sensations
that have no root in reason or knowledge...
just your own or someone else's opinions.

Negative thoughts are only powerful when you believe them.

Once you realize that your negative or fearful thoughts
exist only in your head, they will lose their power over you.

You will always have negative thoughts...
just try not to take them so seriously.

When negative thoughts come knocking at your door,
do not slam the door in their face...
they will only knock harder.

Allow these negative thoughts to *enter your home...*
but *just don't entertain them...*try not to interact with them.

Let them say what they need to...
listen to them and then show them the door.

After all, they are only *thoughts in your head*, and
they will eventually go away.

But sometimes, to prevent a negative downward spiral,
you need a temporary but necessary distraction.

The simplest yet most effective distraction is to
get up and *start moving.*

Get off the couch or out of your chair and and go for a walk.

When your body is at rest,
your mind gets busy thinking or overthinking,
which usually leads to ruminating over negative or harmful thoughts.

When your body is in motion, your excessive thinking decreases,
giving your mind a much needed respite.

So, if you can, go take a walk...preferably outside.

If possible, go on a hike, in the woods...
while there, you can also take delight in the beauty of nature.

The exercise will cause your brain to release endorphins
which will help you to feel better and
feeling good will affect your thoughts in a positive way.

Your negative thoughts are either about something
that has happened (in the past) which,
regardless of how long you ruminate over it,
can never be changed, or
something you are worried about which may
or may not ever happen (in the future).

The past only exists in your memory and
your vision of the future is totally unpredictable,
especially when it's based on a thought that may not even be factual.

Meditation can help you to realize when your mind
is overthinking and it can bring you back to the present moment...
It is *there* where you can let your negative thoughts go.

When you are truly in the present moment,
you are in a place where no negativity can exist.

(See Chapter 15 Meditation & Chapter 24 Living in the Moment)

Of course...
If you are continually struggling with negative thoughts and
feelings, you should absolutely
seek counsel from a mental health professional.

CHAPTER 20

Emotions...Negative and Positive

"Our **emotions** are not made to be
controlled, repressed or shut out...
they are expressions of our humanity
that we need to embrace."
— Unknown

ALL emotions are natural...
ALL emotions serve a purpose.

Feeing both positive and negative emotions are
part of being human.

Emotions aren't necessarily *good* or *bad.*

They are just mental states that allow you to
direct your attention to the events that created them.

Emotions evolved as vital messengers to help us meet
our basic needs for safety and self-preservation.

Your emotions, both positive and negative, have a function.

Negative emotions are there to alert you
that something in your life needs to change...
They encourage you to make those necessary changes.

Positive emotions exist to motivate you to do good things...
They help you to be happy and content.

Of course, you no doubt enjoy having
positive emotions rather than negative ones.

You'd rather be happy than sad...confident instead of insecure.

The key is having a balance of both negative and positive emotions
and because negative emotions are so powerful,
it would be advantageous to your emotional health to have
more positive emotions than negative.

NEGATIVE EMOTIONS

"Negative emotions are a call to action.
They are nature's preferred agent to
inspire change."
— Mark Manson

A negative emotion is an unpleasant or unhappy feeling,
which is evoked in you to express a response
to a negative experience.

It serves a purpose and exists for your benefit.

Negative emotions help you to
remain safe and alive and to motivate you
to make changes to your life.

*Fear, anger, sadness, guilt, loneliness, disgust, frustration,
embarrassment, jealousy, rage, apathy, boredom, disappointment...*
they are all messengers.

Their assignment is to alert you,
to warn you,
to help you realize that
there is a disturbance in your life and that
something needs to change.

Ignoring these negative feelings is
not the healthiest way to deal with them.

That doesn't make them go away...
in fact, the more you resist, the longer they will persist.

A better idea is to befriend your negative emotions.

Make peace with your negative emotions...
stop fighting them...
start listening to them.

Listen to their message or warning,
be appreciative for their advice,
then release them and let them be on their way...
but only after they have served their purpose.

At this point you need to make a decision...
to choose how you will respond to or take action on
the warning from your negative emotion.

When you refuse to embrace your negative feelings,
you are refusing to heal the part of you that triggered
that emotion.

You need to act positively and decisively to
resolve the problem your emotions helped bring to your attention.

If you refuse to change what the uncomfortable emotion
has brought to your attention,
that negative emotion will remain active in your brain...
causing you discomfort...
until you face the situation or circumstance
which this emotion directed you towards.

If you don't take action upon what you have been warned,
your negative emotion will persist long after its useful life...
creating unnecessary negativity in your life.

Human emotions have evolved to be temporary.

It's important to listen to your negative emotions...
What are they alerting you to?

Act appropriately to their warnings and
then take the necessary steps to let them go.

Negative emotions become harmful when they
continue after they have served their purpose or
when they are expressed inappropriately.

Anger can help you fight against problems but
when out-of-control,
can prevent you from seeing clearly.

Fear can help protect you from danger but, when left unchecked
can also prevent you
from seizing good opportunities.

Envy can make you discover what you are denying yourself but
can eventually turn you towards jealousy and bitterness.

When these negative emotions continue beyond their purpose
or usefulness, they can have a *destructive effect* on
your mental, emotional and physical health.

The reason why your negative emotions are so powerful
and can last beyond their useful life is due, in part,
to your inherited 'negativity bias'.

This 'negativity bias', also referred to as
the 'positive-negative asymmetry', as discussed in the previous chapter,
is the tendency to
register negative stimuli more readily than positive stimuli...
feeling the hurt of harsh criticism more powerfully
than the satisfaction of accomplishing an assignment.

Thousands of years ago, when humans lived 'in the wild',
paying constant attention to dangerous threats from wild animals,
as well as from other humans, was necessary for survival.

They had to remain on constant alert for the next danger,
the next attack...

to be on guard, either to 'fight, freeze or flee'
in order to escape danger and remain alive.

These tendencies to pay more attention to the *bad* than to the *good*
were handed down genetically to subsequent generations.

Today, although not faced with the same harsh and dangerous
living conditions, this 'negativity bias'
is still a fundamental part of the nervous system of all humans...
We are all wired with an ancient survival instinct
that evolved to keep our ancestors safe.

Because you have been genetically designed to
defend against the threats and losses in your life,
you unconsciously prioritize the *bad* over the *good.*

You have inherited a powerful survival mechanism...
which was, at one time, critical to remain hyper-vigilant
to survive a dangerous environment.

In today's world, however, that 'negativity bias'
can be counterproductive...
It has a powerful impact on your behavior
and, as we discussed in the previous chapter on
Negative Thoughts, How To Let Them Go,
it is the reason why you

...remember traumatic experiences better
than positive ones
...recall insults better than praise
...react more strongly to negative stimuli
...think about negative things more
frequently than positive ones

Your brain is not conscious of this 'negativity bias' yet
it still utilizes this survival mechanism to keep you safe.

The problem lies in the fact that you most likely do not live
in the same hostile environment as did your ancestors.

Although your brain is just trying to keep you safe,
its emotional responses from this survival mechanism are
far more powerful than they need to be.

Now that you are aware of your tendency towards negativity,
you need to be proactive, taking a mindful approach,
working diligently to concentrate on producing
more positive emotions than negative ones.

The best way to compensate for your brain's 'negativity bias' is to
pay mindful, sustained attention to your daily *positive* experiences...
absorbing them into your brain.

You must try to consciously elevate happier thoughts
to the forefront of your awareness by focusing on and taking in
all the *good* you see throughout your day.

By repeatedly taking in your positive experiences,
you will increase the power of your inner strengths,
your good qualities...
to be prepared to meet life's challenges.

POSITIVE EMOTIONS

Positive emotions help you to *enjoy life*...to be *happy being alive.*

Instead of narrowing your focus, like negative emotions do,
positive emotions affect your brain in
ways that increase your awareness, attention and memory.

They help motivate you to *do good things*...
to make use of your positive character traits.

Positive emotions feel good and they're good for you.

Experiencing positive emotions is vital for you
to lead a happy and healthy life.

Cultivating positive qualities can only lead to
experiencing positive emotions.

(Please See Chapter 16 Your Positive Qualities)

Positive emotions are feelings that we typically
find pleasurable to experience.

They are "pleasant or desirable situational responses...
distinct from pleasurable sensations and
undifferentiated positive affects."
— The Oxford's Handbook of Positive Psychology

Positive emotions are more complex than just simple sensations.

Some common positive emotions include:
Love...Joy...Satisfaction...Contentment...
Interest...Amusement...Happiness...Serenity...Awe

You can increase your positive emotions through
mindfulness meditation...
positive affirmations...
savoring your positive experiences...
cultivating your good character traits.

Building positive emotions is essential,
especially if you're struggling with
persistent negative feelings...such as anger, fear,
frustration or sadness.

Accepting All Your Emotions

All emotions exist to maintain your well-being.

Positive emotions, of course, feel better to you than the negative ones.

If you can accept both your positive and negative feelings
and emotions, they will help support your desire
to lead a safe and healthy, happy and balanced life.

"Positive emotions are here to make you spread good and
negative emotions are here to make you learn.
Accept both and handle them with care."
— A. Krishna

Antidotes to Destructive, Negative Emotions

"Any person capable of angering you
becomes your master."
— Epictetus

Emotions evolved as necessary messengers to help us
meet our basic needs for self-preservation and safety.

For example...
Fear of danger helps us to be on guard against any
threats to our safety...
Feeling disgusted by something toxic serves as
a protection against being poisoned.

However...
when these negative emotions extend beyond their useful life,
they can become harmful, injurious and destructive.

When you have a destructive, negative emotion...
it's usually *impulsive* and based on
misconceptions and *illogical reasoning.*

Emotions become destructive when they are
expressed inappropriately.

The ***antidote*** to an unhealthy, destructive negative emotion is a
positive, constructive emotion...
one that is *realistic* and grounded in *valid observation*
and *reasoning.*

To reduce anger, hatred and fear,
you need to cultivate patience, tolerance, compassion and love.

The effect of developing constructive emotions
is a calm and peaceful state of mind.

Positive emotions are the foundation of your
emotional immune system...
your emotional intelligence.

Positive states of mind can act as antidotes to
your negative tendencies.

Because your thoughts have a direct and significant affect
on your emotions, you need to focus on *positive thinking...*
then, with the help of a positive emotional antidote,
you can reduce your destructive negative emotion.

(Please see Chapter 18 Your Thoughts and Positive Thinking)

Strategies for releasing most Destructive Negative Emotions are:

Do not try to resist them or they will persist.

Allow them to "pass through" your mind

Intentionally Focus on Positive Thoughts and Emotions

Utilize your Positive Qualities, your Inner Strengths

Use your Positive Affirmations

Practice a Mindfulness or Loving-Kindness Meditation

Stay focused on Living in the Present Moment

To the extent you can, try replacing destructive, negative emotions
with positive, beneficial ones.

Negative emotions are much more powerful than positive ones.

Therefore it would be wise then,
to cultivate many more positive emotions
than negative ones.

And always remember that eventually,
no matter what your negative emotion is...
It Will Pass !!!

Overthinking... Dwelling on the Past Worrying About Things Out of Your Control Being Anxious About the Future

"All negativity is caused by an
accumulation of psychological time and
denial of the present. Unease, anxiety,
tension, stress, worry - all forms of fear -
are caused by too much future, and not
enough presence. Guilt, regret,
resentment, grievances, sadness,
bitterness, and all forms
of non-forgiveness are caused by too
much past, and not enough presence."
— E Tolle

Never allow the sadness of your past nor the fear of your future to diminish the happiness of your present.

You have made mistakes in your past that you may not be proud of... *everyone has.*

You are *not* your mistakes...you are much more.

Do not let your mistakes define you.

Do not let memories of those mistakes hinder your recovery.
Do not let them prevent you from staying true to
your commitments - *to remain sober,*
work towards improving your lifestyle and
pursue happiness and contentment.

Guilt, shame and resentment have no place in the present.

Do not hold on to them...Let them go!

Overthinking is thinking too much...
needlessly, passively, endlessly
and excessively contemplating the meanings, causes and
consequences of your character, your emotions and your
problems.

It is repetitive, unproductive thought.

Overthinking is thinking about the same situation over and
over again without ever coming close to a solution or conclusion.

It is a prison that holds you back and prevents you from
taking action.

Overthinking will destroy your mood as well as your happiness...
It lets you believe that everything is worse than it really is.

Take a deep breath, exhale and have faith...
What's meant to be, will be.

Overthinking falls into two categories...

Rumination - dwelling over something that happened in the ***past...***
something that can never be changed.

Stop replaying unfortunate situations from your past...
That will only perpetuate your anger and sadness.

and

Worry - fretting over something that may or may not happen in the ***future...***

It will never change tomorrow's troubles but it can take from you, today's peace.

The Past

♫ "Don't let the past remind us
of what we are not now." ♫
— Crosby, Stills & Nash

The past is only kept alive through your memories and emotional feelings, both positive and negative.

The past is *what was...*
There is no need to dwell on it...
Just learn from it and move forward.

The past is *in* the past...
It does not exist any longer.

No amount of thoughts, regrets or resentments can change it.

No amount of guilt can alter the past.

You need to give up the *What ifs...*
What if I did this or What if I did that?

Reliving your regretful past over and over, can only serve to torture your mind and you don't deserve that...No one does.

Only *forgiveness* of others and yourself
can release the negativity from your past.

It frees up your mind to be here, in the present...
where life is happening...
the only place where life really happens.

Overthinking usually occurs when you are self-focused, self-critical
and preoccupied with the fact that you are unhappy...
obsessing over the causes, meanings and consequences
of your unhappiness.
It is when you are overly concerned with regrets and disappointments
from the past
accompanied by feelings of loss, failure and hopelessness.

It is time now, to say goodbye to all the negativity from your past.

Anxiety About the Future

Life today is very uncertain...
so it's normal to have concerns about your future.

Anticipatory anxiety is not uncommon...
it is the excessive worry about future events that may or
may not happen,
assuming that the outcome will be to your detriment.

It is a fear or worry that something bad may happen...
focusing on something you cannot predict or control.

Unless your worrying motivates you to begin a plan of action,
it serves absolutely no purpose.

"If a problem is fixable, if a situation is
such that you can do something about it,
then there is no need to worry.
If it is not fixable, then there is no help in
worrying whatsoever."
— Dalai Lama

No amount of worrying about anything can ever change the outcome.

Worrying about things in the future doesn't stop them
from happening...it just takes away from your happiness today.

Chronic anxiety about the future can cause you undue stress
and could negatively affect your well-being.

Worry is concerned with the possibility of danger, harm or pain
from something that has not happened and never may.

Reduce Your Overthinking

There are a number of things you can do to
challenge your *overthinking.*

Practice *mindfulness* - with mindfulness, you experience
each moment of life for all that it is,
instead of letting your thoughts overwhelm you.

Distraction – distract yourself by *doing something...*
Reading, taking a walk, singing a song, listening to music,
exercising.

Question your thoughts -
Are they accurate?
Are they real?
Are they exaggerated?

Talk to someone - a friend, a family member
or a therapist.

The most effective and long term solution to reduce
your overthinking, is to *start living more in the present.*

(Please see Chapter 24 Living in the Present)

CHAPTER 23

Training Your Brain

Neural plasticity refers to the *plastic-like*
or *malleable* nature of the brain.

It other words...
your brain can be *shaped* or *molded...*
It can change...it is always changing.

Your mind, your brain and your body are interconnected as
an ingenious system to safeguard homeostasis,
(the maintaining of stable conditions in your mind and body)
for your survival.

Neural plasticity is the ability of neural networks in the brain
to change through growth and reorganization...
your neural pathways make new connections.

You have the *power* to change your brain...
to change your thinking...
to *train* your brain
through self directed neural plasticity.

You can change your brain by *training* your brain,
which in turn, will change your mind
to focus on what you really want and really need...
a positive and happy life.

Your mind takes its shape from what it rests upon...
what you give your attention to.

Your brain is adaptable,
continually remodeling itself from your new experiences.

By your learning and practicing new ways of thinking,
you can create new connections between the neurons
in your brain.

The more you practice, the stronger the connections become.

Repetition rewires the brain...
Doing anything repeatedly creates a pattern...
Patterns create neural pathways (connections in your brain,
kind of like information highways).

By repeatedly taking in new, positive information,
by focusing on and
remembering positive experiences,
your brain forms new neural pathways,
which create new positive beliefs and habits.

You are hardwiring your brain...
training your brain to increase your happiness.

Positivity leads to Happiness.

The more you focus on the positive, (repeating affirmations,
meditating often and savoring and reflecting on
your daily positive experiences)
the more you help strengthen your brain's new neural pathways,
which can transform your new thought patterns,
your new beliefs and behaviors.

At the same time, the neural connections along your old
pathways of negativity will start to break down and fall
away with disuse.

This means that you have the potential to
create a new and different life...
a life with more positivity and less negativity.

Your brain will function according to the ways you teach it.

You can gradually counter any negative thoughts and feelings you may have just by focusing on the positive.

You are literally reshaping your brain's nerve cells...
training your brain to *increase feelings of happiness.*

It works the same way with learning a new language or
a musical instrument...
The more you practice, (through *repetition*) the easier it becomes
to speak "Hungarian" or play the "Harpsichord"...
eventually you begin to consciously think less about each word
or each note and just speak or play without much thought.

Repetition creates long term memory by eliciting
strong chemical interactions at the synapses of the neurons
in your brain, which strengthens your neural pathways.

New neural pathways are the basis for new habits
through the repetition and practice of thinking,
feeling and acting.

With enough repetition, over time, it becomes automatic...
you become conditioned.

Your brain is ever-changing, (neural plasticity) reconfiguring
its wiring based on your new thoughts, new emotions and
new experiences.

Your brain is adaptable...
it designs new combinations of nerve cells and neurotransmitters,
creating new neural pathways, in response to new input.

You can systematically train your mind by what you
deliberately select and focus on

...by using Positive Affirmations – verbally expressing
positive thoughts until, with confidence in them,
you allow them to affect you emotionally.

...by writing down the things in life that you are grateful for,
helping your brain absorb more positivity.

...by appreciating and savoring your good experiences.

...by practicing Mindfulness Meditation.

Continue using your mind to change your brain with positivity...
creating a more positive and happy you!

CHAPTER 24

Living in the Present Moment

"The secret of health for both mind and
body is not to mourn for the past, worry
about the future, or anticipate troubles,
but to live in the present moment wisely
and earnestly." – Buddha

There is only ever *this moment...*
Life is *always Now...*
Your entire life unfolds in this
Constant Now...
Life is only available in *The Present.*

The *past* only exists through your memories...
the *future*, through anticipation...
but only by thinking of them *in the present.*

The *present moment* is all you are really guaranteed.

Living in *the present moment* or
the here and now,
means that you are aware and mindful of what is happening
at *this very moment,*
focused on or centered in *the here and now.*

Do you habitually fail to enjoy, savor
and live in *the present* moment because your mind is someplace else?
...postponing your happiness?
...believing that what counts most will happen in the future?
...convincing yourself that tomorrow will be better than today?

Do you constantly miss opportunities happening in *the present*?
...dwelling on things that already happened, in the past?
...wondering what could have or should have occurred?
...imagining how different your life might be today?

If you worry about *what might be* and
wonder *what might have been,*
you might miss out on *what really is.*

As you focus on becoming more accepting and more peaceful
with where you are, *in the moment,*
rather than where you *think* you should be,
you will find peace and contentment right where you are,
in the present,
which is the only time that really exists.

If you can be fully engaged in
the present moment,
you will have less reason to dwell on any fears or anxieties...
you will be too busy enjoying the beauty and wonder of life.

Fears and anxieties do not and cannot exist
in *the present moment.*

When you live in *the present moment,*
you develop concentration...
you become empowered.

The present is the only time when you have any power.

To a large extent, your happiness and peace of mind
are based on your ability to *live* in *the present moment.*

The quality of your life greatly increases with a
present moment or
moment-to-moment awareness of each little thing.

The ability to *savor* the positive experiences of your life is one of
the most important ingredients of happiness and contentment.

(Please See Chapter 28 Slow Down and Savor the Good)

You have a much greater chance at a happy and content life
by deliberately choosing what to think about.

You need to start living in *the present moment* and
stop dwelling on the past and worrying about the future.

Find your happiness *now*, in *the present moment...*
because your tomorrow may never come.

Living in the present helps you reduce
fears from your mind...
your concern over something that may or may not happen,
in the future.

Living in the present moment is about
living your life consciously, with acceptance and mindfulness
of what is happening right now...
letting go or not being distracted
by your thoughts about the past or the future.

(Please See Chapter 26 Acceptance, Chapter 25 Mindfulness
and Chapter 27 Letting Go)

When you *live in the present,*
all of your attention is focused on *the present moment,*
right where you are.

You cannot relive the past...
nor can you experience the future before it arrives...
but in between the two, there exists
the only time there ever is...*the present.*

The present is the point between the past and the future...
It is a point with no time...
and yet everything that ever happens, happens in *the present moment.*

"If you were conscious, that is to say
totally *present* in the *Now,* all negativity

would dissolve almost instantly...It could
not survive in your presence."
— E. Tolle

When you are suffering, anxious or unhappy,
stay *in the present*...in the now.

Unhappiness and problems cannot survive in the now.

When you are aware and *present*,
you are not caught up obsessing about your past,
nor are you having anticipatory anxiety about the future.

Realistically, there are, of course, certain times when you
need to recall things from your past,
to look back on past successes and mistakes and learn from them
and
there are times when you need to consider the future,
in order to make any necessary preparations.

The key is to
have a balance of
past, present and future with
the majority of your time being spent, absorbed *in the present*
because that is where you always are.

"Living in the present moment creates
the experience of eternity."
— Deepak Chopra

Truly *living in the present* can give you
the sense of living forever...you find eternity in every moment.

Being present minded or living in the here-and-now
just might be the key to your happiness...
It has certainly worked for me!

Staying *present* puts your life in perspective...
keeping you grounded and connected to all that matters.

The best way to really *live in the present,*
is to practice Mindfulness and
the best place to learn how to *live in the present* is in Nature.

Why not combine the two and take a *mindful walk* in *the woods*
or along a quiet beach or in a city park.

Try to notice, feel and absorb the beauty of the
natural surroundings with all of your senses.

You cannot help but *be present, while mindfully* walking in nature.

(Please see Chapter 38 Nature and Hiking in Nature)

Sadness and bitterness, guilt and regret, grievances and resentments
are just remnants from your past...
let them go so you can start living in the *present.*

Anxiety and tension, fear and worry, stress and nervousness
only exist when your mind is in the future.

Bring your mind back to the present, where it belongs.

"Life is a great and wondrous mystery
and the only thing we know that we have
for sure is what is right here, right now.
Don't miss it." — Leo Buscaglia

Today is life...Right Now is life...
Life is a succession of moments...
Live each and every one of them.

Consider very young children...
they have no concept of past or future...
they live *in the present* only and
they appear to be enjoying it with so much
joy and happiness.

Living in the Present is really the only place where you can find
your joy, your happiness and your contentment.

(Please See Chapter 31 Happiness, Contentment and Inner Peace)

Live like today is the first day of your life...
after all, It Really Is!!!

CHAPTER 25

Mindfulness

Mindfulness

"We live in forgetfulness. But always there is the opportunity to live our life fully. When we drink water, we can be aware that we are drinking water. When we walk, we can be aware that we are walking. Mindfulness is available to us in every moment."
— Thich Nhat Hanh

What Mindfulness is Not

Mindfulness is **not** a religion...
although it does owe its roots to Eastern religions, philosophies and traditions.

There **is** a Mindfulness Meditation but Mindfulness itself, is **not** a meditation.

It's **not** about emptying your mind of thought...
Instead, mindfulness allows you to be in harmony with your thoughts and feelings.

Mindfulness is **not** an escape from pain...however, it *can* help people who suffer with chronic pain.

It is **not** a way to relax, although it can help to reduce your stress.

Mindfulness is **not** something you *do... It's a way of being.*

What Mindfulness Is

"The best way to capture moments is to
pay attention. This is how we cultivate
mindfulness. Mindfulness means being
awake. It means knowing what you are
doing."
— Jon Kabat Zinn

Mindfulness is your ability to be *Fully Present...*
to be aware of where you are and what you are doing...
not overreacting...
not overwhelmed by what's going on around you.

Mindfulness is *awareness*
consciousness
wakefulness

It is the *awareness* that arises from paying attention
on purpose, in the present moment,
non-judgmentally, to things as they are.

It is the practice of *deliberately paying attention,*
conscious of your thoughts and feelings, your bodily sensations
and your surrounding environment.

Mindfulness is a different way of looking at the world...
You just notice, observe and accept.

Mindfulness is non-judgmental observation...
wakefulness and impartial watchfulness...
observing without criticizing.

Although it is non-judgmental, it is curious and compassionate...
encouraging awareness of any thoughts, feelings or sensations
you are presently experiencing.

It treats all experiences, thoughts and feelings equally...
nothing is repressed or suppressed...
You see things as they really are...adding nothing to perception...
subtracting nothing...distorting nothing.

It is non-conceptual awareness...observing everything
as if it were occurring for the first time.

You become immersed in what is happening in the moment...
without criticism or judgment...
without wishing for things to be any different from what they are.

Mindfulness is knowing what you are thinking when you are thinking it...
Knowing what you are feeling when you are feeling it.

With mindfulness, you become more aware of where you are and
what you're doing,
without becoming overly reactive or overwhelmed
by what's going on around you.

It helps you create a space between yourself and your reactions,
and that helps you to wisely respond rather than prematurely react.

With mindfulness you can experience a moment of life for all it is,
instead of allowing your thoughts
to take you where you weren't planning on going.

Mindfulness helps you to spend more time in the present moment.

It helps you to live in a world without stressing about
the past or the future...
living in the "right now" with no regrets, guilt, bitterness,
self-recrimination, dread or anxiety.

It's about openly embracing the present moment...
increasing your attention and awareness there.

When you're fully immersed in the present,
you can savor the unique quality of each moment.

It lets you see that life consists of moments and that
each precious moment is all we have.

The only thing that is real, in any way,
is the here and now...
It's all you have and it's all you need.

You are always in the present...isn't that where your mind should be?

Mindfulness is about being aware of your thoughts
without judging them
or trying to suppress them.

With sustained mindfulness, you can explore what happens when
your thoughts and emotions are allowed to come and go
in awareness...
with a non-judgmental attitude.

It helps you to be aware of your negative thought patterns and
not be overwhelmed by them,
knowing that they are just thoughts, nothing more and nothing less.

Mindfulness refines your attention so that you can connect, fully
and directly, with whatever life brings.

You can *choose* to pay attention to what really brings you happiness.

Mindfulness enables you to cultivate a different quality of attention,
where you can relate to what you see before you,
not just as an echo of the past or a foreshadowing of the future,
but more *as it is right now.*

You become more in touch with life *as it is*
when you allow yourself to experience life through your senses
rather than through your unexamined and habitual thoughts.

Mindfulness is *non-reactionary*...
instead of reacting to the events in your life,
you are more in control...you can respond wisely and appropriately.

You don't allow outside circumstances to influence you.

You can observe the uncomfortable feelings your brain creates
and not react.

This becomes your new, more peaceful way of dealing with your life...
putting you in control of your new life.

Mindfulness isn't meant to eliminate your thinking...
it allows you to *watch* your thoughts...
to observe how one leads to another and then you decide...
whether you need to let go or
change the direction of your thinking.

Mindfulness is about saying yes to life...
accepting reality, just as it is.

The harder you struggle against reality,
the more unhappiness you will create.

Seeing reality as it really is, allows you to make wise decisions.

In essence, mindfulness is about being

...Awake, Aware and In the Present Moment
...Observant but Non-Judgmental
...Being In Control and Non-Reactionary
...Accepting and Non-Critical

And the benefits of practicing mindfulness are many.

Mindfulness

...Promotes Well-Being

...Makes you more Resilient
...Increases your Energy Level
...Helps Manage Negative Emotions
...Decreases your Stress and Anxiety
...Increases your Happiness
...Improves your Sleep
...Increases your Emotional and Physical Health

Mindfulness Meditation

With mindfulness, all you're trying to do is to
pay attention to the present moment
without any judgment.

Your mind will wander...thoughts will arise.
Your mind will drift to something that has happened or
something you anticipate will happen.

That is nothing to fear...that is human nature.

The moment you recognize that your mind has wandered,
you can then bring it back to the present moment.

The more this occurs, whether in meditation or your daily life,
the easier it will become to be mindful.

If you have judging thoughts, let them pass.

Just return your attention to the present moment.

Mindfulness is the practice of returning, again and again,
to the present moment.

In meditation, use the sensation of your breath to anchor you
to the present moment.

Every time you do this, you reinforce your ability to do it again.

By practicing Mindfulness Meditation, it helps you to
remain mindful throughout the day.

Meditation is the perfect place and time to practice *mindfulness.*
It encourages you to slow down and realize the benefits
of *mindfulness.*

It allows you time to suspend judgment towards your thoughts by
refocusing on your breath - your focal point.

You're not aiming for mindlessness by wiping away
your constant thinking.

You are just practicing refocusing or bringing your attention
back to your breath when you notice it has wandered.

The ultimate goal of *mindfulness meditation* is to achieve a
state of *alertness...*
being intensely aware of what you are experiencing in the moment
without any interpretation or judgment.

Learning mindfulness meditation is straightforward enough
to practice on your own.

You are ready to begin now, just as you are.

Keep in mind, meditation is a practice, so it is never perfect.

Find a place that feels calm and quiet.

There is no specific posture...just get comfortable,
either sitting, standing, kneeling, or lying down.

There are just three basic things to remember...

One) Focus on your breath...
be aware of your breath...
follow the sensation of your breath as it flows in and out.

Two) Notice your thoughts...
do not ignore, suppress or resist them...

Acknowledge that they are there and that they are just thoughts...
Try to remain calm and become comfortable with your thoughts...
As all things in life are impermanent, they too, will
eventually float away...

However, if staying with a thought becomes too difficult,
if you are feeling anxious or worried, go back to the breath...
Use it as your anchor or refuge.

Three) Give yourself a break...
be kind to your wandering mind...
The practice of refocusing or retuning to your breath is,
in fact, what *mindfulness* is.

As you continue to regularly practice mindfulness, your ability to
center yourself will improve,
allowing you time to cultivate your inherent positive qualities or
inner resources, leading to feelings of calm and contentment.

The continual focusing and refocusing on your breath
will allow any feelings of anxiety or depression to wane,
while boosting your feelings of empathy and connectivity.

"Mindfulnesses is simply being aware of
what is happening right now without
wishing it were different...
Enjoying the pleasant without holding on
when it changes (which it will)...
Being with the unpleasant without feeling
it will always be this way (which it won't).
— James Baraz

By practicing mindfulness, you will create a new consciousness
that positively affects how you think, feel
and interact with the world around you.

Acceptance... Accepting What You Can't Change

"Understanding is the first step to
acceptance, and only with **Acceptance**
can there be recovery."
— J.K. Rowling

Unhappiness comes from your unwillingness to **accept** life
as being *different* from your expectations.

But life doesn't usually provide you with fairytale endings, does it.

In fact, life will *never* be exactly the way you want it to be...
You don't always get what you want...
Accept that!

So, what does acceptance actually mean and
why is choosing it **beneficial** for you?

Well first of all, Acceptance is *not* resignation or passivity.

It is *not* weakness...
it takes courage to face reality when it's not in your favor.

Acceptance is *not* quitting...
it is shifting your focus and attention from what you cannot change
to what you can.

Acceptance is about saying *yes* to life,
just *as it is.*

The well known Serenity Prayer encourages you to
"...accept the things you cannot change".

Acceptance of what you can't change is especially critical
to your recovery.

Acceptance is the coming to terms with the fact that there exists
some things that are beyond your control, such as

...Events from the past
...Things that others say or do
...What others think of you
...Thoughts that pass through your mind
...Things that may or may not happen in the future

As opposed to those things you have control over

...Your words
...Your actions
...How you treat others
...Your choices
...Your decisions
...The amount of effort you put forth
...How you handle your feelings
...The way you care for yourself

Acceptance *doesn't mean* liking, wanting, condoning, agreeing with,
choosing or supporting something...
It's knowing that resisting or rejecting, may cause you
unnecessary suffering.

Acceptance is part of mindfulness or being mindful...
perceiving your experience and just acknowledging it
rather than judging it as being either good or bad.

You can practice acceptance towards
...your current experience
...your thoughts or emotions
...your past
...your health or appearance

...others' opinions or beliefs
...yourself

You are *just recognizing* the reality that some things cannot be changed, at least not at this present time.

However, by accepting your situation in the present, it does not preclude you from working on trying to change it, in the future.

The Oxford English Dictionary defines 'acceptance' as "a *willingness* to tolerate a difficult situation".

Acceptance is a *willful* act.
It is
...a choice you make
...not a fleeting thought
...a solid commitment

Ultimately the only things you are going to be able to control are your own actions, choices and decisions.

When you switch your focus in that direction, you'll be spending less time worrying about the things you cannot control.

Acceptance is:
...tolerant
...open-minded
...unprejudiced
...patient
...understanding

As you begin to live with greater acceptance, you will notice an increase of your joy, your happiness and your contentment.

Your inner peace will increase when you understand and accept the inevitable problems of life.

You will be able to maintain a calm mental and emotional state.

"Acceptance of what has happened is the first step to
overcoming the consequences of any misfortune."
— William James

I'm sure, as we all do, you get frustrated when you
cannot change a situation to meet your expectations.

And there will always be people, circumstances and events
that you find disagreeable and are not able to change.

Accepting what you don't agree with is one of the most
difficult aspects in sobriety that you will face.

So... what can you do about it?

"When we can no longer change our
situation we are challenged to
change ourselves."
— Viktor Frankl

It is challenging to make changes to your life,
but when you finally do make the necessary changes,
you will begin to reap the rewards...
benefits such as having:

...a more positive attitude
...less stress and worrying
...the ability to accept change
...greater appreciation and gratitude

You can change or transform your life by making the
willful choice of acceptance.

Essentially, acceptance is an act of kindness to yourself...
it is a part of practicing self-compassion.

A lack of acceptance of what you realistically cannot change
will lead to frustration and disappointment...
unnecessary emotions that can negatively affect
your new sober lifestyle.

To accept something you cannot change may require you to
make an *attitude adjustment*..

As you progress in your sobriety,
you will continue to transform your life...
making adjustments to the good, when necessary.

Focus on what you **can do** about a given situation...
If you cannot change something,
then accept the reality of it.

"Whatever the present moment contains,
accept it as if you had chosen it.
Always work with it not against it...
All you really need to do is accept this
moment fully. You are then at ease in the
here and now and at ease with yourself."
— Eckhart Tolle

With *acceptance,* your transformation towards the positive
will be the journey of your life...
it will keep you on the path of happiness and sobriety.

"Happiness can only exist in acceptance."
— George Orwell

CHAPTER 27

Letting Go

"One of the hardest lessons in life is
letting go...whether it's guilt, anger,
love, loss or betrayal...Change is
never easy...We fight to hold on and
we fight to let go."
— Unknown

Let go of the way you think it should be and **accept** what is.

When you **let go** of your problems, instead of fighting or
resisting them, your life will begin to flow.

You can **let go** or release negative beliefs, thoughts, emotions,
behaviors, patterns and habits...
through meditation, mindfulness, affirmations,
positive thinking and actions.

Let go, by...
dropping thoughts, words and deeds that cause suffering and harm...
yielding rather than breaking...
surrendering to what is, even if it's not your choice...
accepting the impermanent nature of existence.

Let go of...
resentment, resistance, unhealthy relationships and
the negativity from your past...

The longer you hold on to the baggage from your past,
the heavier it feels and the more it weighs you down.

“Letting go isn’t about forgetting…
it’s about learning and moving on.
It’s making a choice to be strengthened
by your past, not strangled by it.”
— Steve Maraboli

Your bag of mental reminders of mistakes and losses
is only preventing you from enjoying your happiness in the present.

Your load of negativity from the past…what is it good for?

Absolutely Nothing!

What happened in your past has passed…
you can never change what has already happened.

Learn from it…
Accept it…
Drop It…
Lose It…
Let It Go!

One of the most *freeing* moments in life is when you find
the courage to *let go* of what you cannot change.

Let go of all the things that you don’t need…
things that are holding you back or
tying you down…
Why hang on to something that has no benefit for you and
can only do you harm?

Focus on what you *can* control and let go of what you *cannot.*

The Serenity Prayer says:
“May I have the serenity to accept the
things I cannot change, the courage to
change the things I can, and the wisdom
to know the difference.”

In other words:
You need to *change* the changeable,
accept the unchangeable,
and *remove yourself* from the unacceptable...

If it's out of your hands, it deserves freedom from your mind as well.

You need to **Let go** of...

*listening to negative thoughts and believing that they're true

*worrying about what happened in the past

*worrying about what might happen in the future

*being pessimistic

*always expecting the worst

*allowing your emotions to control your actions

*the need to always be right

*the need to fit in

* living your life for the weekend

*your limiting beliefs

*putting too much pressure on yourself

*disapproving of yourself or putting yourself down

*the things that don't make you happy

*always trying to please everyone

*the need to impress others

*worrying about what others think of you

*overthinking

*what you cannot change

*always having to be perfect

*judging others

*judging yourself

*unrealistic expectations

*blaming others for your problems

*comparing yourself to others

*complaining

*excuses

*your self-doubt

*your fear of failure

*your guilt

*your pride

*holding grudges

*your jealousy

*your anger

*your unhealthy and destructive relationships

*criticizing yourself

*criticizing others

*refusing to change

*who you think you're supposed to be

Let go of all that makes you weak.

"Sometimes *letting things go* is an act of far greater power than defending or hanging on."
— Eckhart Tolle

It may take all your courage and strength but you need to...
Let go of all that *unnecessary negativity* and open yourself to your new sober and happy lifestyle.

Let go of all the things that stop you from growing and becoming a better person.

Letting go is not about losing hope...
it's about hoping for more, hoping for something better, for something worth holding on to.

It's a great feeling when you recognize all of the things that just don't matter anymore and let them go.

Slow Down and Savor the Good

Slowing Down

♫ "**Slow down**, you move too fast. You
gotta make the morning last. Just
kicking down the cobblestones.
Lookin for fun and feeling groovy." ♫
— The 59th Street Bridge Song
By Simon and Garfunkel

We live in a society where people are always busy and in a hurry...
always trying to keep up with everything...
trying to get as much done as they possibly can,
yet always running behind.

Believing this will bring them happiness, they get caught up in
a fiercely competitive struggle for wealth and power.

They sacrifice their most valuable commodity – **time** –
for a disproportionate financial reward.

They find themselves trapped in a competitive and
exhausting **rat race**.

Wanting to keep up with everyone else, they are constantly
rushing and hurrying around...
aways feeling like they're falling behind schedule,
running late or out of time...
sadly missing out on the things that really matter...
living and seeing life as one big blur.

Most people don't have time to even
see the roses,
let alone smell them.

On the other hand, **slowing down** will make you
more aware of your surroundings...
to see where you are and what is happening...
to be aware of what really matters and what you really need.

It will help you to be more mindful...
experiencing moments of peacefulness.

Slowing down can help towards achieving peace of mind...
a state of mental and emotional balance and calm...
a quiet mind, free from worries, fears or stresses.

And it will help keep you on the path of happiness and
contentment, one of your three commitments.

While alcohol obscures the clarity and depth of your mind,
slowing down can help you focus better and
bring a calmness to your mind...
improving your mental and emotional well-being.

You will think more clearly and act accordingly...
making wiser decisions.

Going slower will actually help you to go further.

It will begin to feel like you have more time for yourself...
You will.

And that's a good thing,
because time is the most valuable resource that you can ever have.

When you slow down,
you begin noticing things, enabling you
to be more sensitive to your emotional and physical needs.

Life will be calmer and
your thinking slower and more orderly,
if you just slow down and do one thing at a time.

Before each task, take a few deep breaths...
your thinking will slow to a more manageable pace.

You will soon begin to realize that by purposely slowing down,
you now have more control over your mind.

Slowing down will help you to be more mindful and
be able to react to situations
in a nonjudgmental manner.

You will become more aware of your surroundings...
mindfully observing exactly what is there...
no more and no less.

Slowing Down allows you to be more present and
helps to reduce your stress and anxiety.

You will begin to experience greater calm and more positivity.

And slowing down is essential both for *living in the present*
as well as for *meditation.*

(Please See Chapter 24 Living in the Present Moment and Chapter 15
Meditation)

> "Just slow down.
> Slow down your speech.
> Slow down your breathing.
> Slow down your walking.
> Slow down your eating.
> Let this slower, steadier pace
> perfume your mind...
> just fill your mind."
> — Doko

Does racing about make you happy or
do you feel more stressed and worn out?

Slow Down...you will look more
confident,
rested,
dignified and happy.

It's your life, no one else's....
Slow Down and Enjoy It!!!

Savoring the Good

"Savor each moment as it passes,
embrace all that life has to offer and
celebrate the joy of every day."
— Papyrus

Savoring refers to the capacity to *attend to*, *appreciate* and *enhance* the positive experiences of your life...
to experience something good,
slowly...
in order for you to enjoy it as much as possible.

Try to view it as if you were seeing it for the first time.

Learn to *live in the present* and enjoy the gift of each moment without waiting for the next one.

Learn to let go of those distractions and outside demands that can absorb your time and
disallow you the critical time you need to slow down and savor the things you find joy in.

It's about allowing yourself to find joy, feel joy and live joyously...
the use of your thoughts and actions to increase the *intensity*,
duration and *appreciation* of your positive experiences and emotions.

Enjoy a positive experience as much as you can...
using your thoughts, feelings and behaviors to *intensify*
and *prolong* that enjoyable experience.

Try to sustain any pleasurable moments you have and
deliberately store them in your mind.

In other words:
Whenever you have a good feeling,
hang on to it for as long as you possibly can...
Savor it...Think on it...Let it lead into a positive upward spiral.

Making time and taking time to slow down and savor the things
you enjoy can really enhance your sense of well-being.

And slowing down, itself, will bring with it a number of benefits,
including, having greater clarity, making better decisions and
helping you to manage your emotions, which is a requirement for
your **new sober lifestyle.**

Savoring requires a deliberate, mindful awareness of
the present moment.

Slowing down to savor the moment is a natural way to
increase your gratitude.

(Please see Chapter 33 Gratitude)

It is a powerful tool for boosting positivity and adding to or
increasing your happiness and contentment.

"I fall in love everyday with new songs,
dogs, scents, pieces of art, illusions,
five minute conversations, a sunset in
my rear view mirror, a story, a daydream.
What a pleasure it is."
— Victoria Erickson

If you enjoy what is before you,
in the present,
it will increase your appreciation of what
you already have,
rather than wanting what you don't have.

It's kind of difficult to be all stressed out when you're aware of
all the positivity that surrounds you *in the present.*

Savor the moment,
notice what's going on right here,
right now and
appreciate it...   Treasure it!

It's about taking time to notice and appreciate all the little things
that lead to greater happiness and reduced stress.

Savoring involves *mindfulness*...intentionally attending to
present moment experiences that
contribute to your positive feelings and emotional health.

Along with self-compassion and *living in the present moment,*
savoring too can serve to counteract your ruminating about
the past or your anxiety over the future.

When you find pleasure in life,
it doesn't mean that you're ignoring the things that are hard or painful.

What you're doing is just opening up to the wonderful things
that exist all around you.

Bask in them.
Luxuriate in them.
Take Delight in them.

Marinate yourself in the daily pleasures of life with all of your senses.

Slowing Down to savor sights, sounds, smells, tastes and
physical feelings not only extends your positive experiences
but helps keep you in *the present moment.*

Savor...
the beauty that you see...
the music that you hear...
the aromas you smell...
the delicious foods that you taste...
the warmth of a hug...
petting your little, furry friend...
all the beauty that nature has provided for you to see.

Because of your inherent 'negativity bias', you will need to
continually focus on drawing the positive into your life.

Savoring, taking notice of a good or happy experience
purposely trying to extend its positive effects,
appreciating it for as long as possible is one way to do that.

Savor the moment...Celebrate it...Absorb it...Extend it!

Finding joy in savoring things can increase your inner strengths,
which will help you to face some of life's challenges,
thereby helping your resolve to remain faithful to your all important
Three Commitments —

Remaining Sober
Maintaining a Healthy Lifestyle
Continuing on Your Path of Happiness

Forgiveness... forgiving others

"It is not an easy journey to get to a place
where you forgive people...But it is such a
powerful place because it frees you."
— Tyler Perry

Forgiveness is a highly recommended course of action on your journey of happiness and sobriety.

You no doubt, have had people in your life that have offended you or harmed you in some way.

Are there some that you have not forgiven?

Are you still holding on to grudges, carrying bitterness, anger or resentment?

Allowing yourself to remain angered can only destroy *your* peace of mind...
Harboring feelings of hatred and resentment will cause a disturbance in your mind that will imprison you in an unhappy mental state.

Letting go of grudges and bitterness is to remove a heavy emotional burden you have been carrying...
It will make way for improved mental, emotional and physical health, allowing you to enjoy peace of mind.

You need to forgive people...
not because they deserve to be forgiven but
because you need to close the door to the negativity of your past.

Forgiving others is a present to yourself.

Forgive them...
not because they deserve forgiveness,
but because you deserve peace.

It is not something you do for others...
It is something you do for yourself...
so you can move forward.

The weak can never forgive...
Forgiveness takes courage...
It is an attribute of the strong.

Forgiving is not forgetting the pain that was caused...
It is remembering the pain without the anger.

It is of no benefit to you to hold on to anger, resentment and pain.

Make peace with the pain and
let go of your anger and resentment.

"To be wronged is nothing, unless you
continue to remember it."
— Confucius

Holding on to anger only hurts *you*...
you and *you* alone.

When you let go of the anger and resentment you begin to heal.

The only way you can eliminate the negativity from your past
and still retain the memories of your positive experiences
is through forgiveness.

It's not about accepting, condoning or excusing someone's behavior.

It's about letting it go and preventing their behavior from
destroying your peace of mind.

There will always, always, always be someone who will
disappoint you or hurt you in some way.

For you to be happy, you need to learn to forgive,
to let go and to move on with your life.

"Forgiveness is simply about
understanding that every one of us is
both inherently good and inherently
flawed. Within every hopeless situation and
every seemingly hopeless person lies the
possibility of transformation."
— Desmond Tutu

Forgiveness is another word for freedom...
freedom to *love again...*
to *laugh again...*
to *live* again.

It's making a conscious decision to *live in the present*
and put the past to rest.

Forgive...
to heal your mind and spirit...
to let go of negativity...
to move on with your life...
for peace of mind...
to feel better and feel happy.

Forgiving will most certainly help you to heal and to continue on your transformational journey of happiness and sobriety,
remembering your commitments to

1. Remain Sober
2. Change Your Lifestyle
3. Seek Happiness and Contentment

"Forgiveness isn't approving what
happened. It's choosing to rise above it."
— Robin Sharma

Forgive what has happened...so you may enjoy what is about to.

CHAPTER 30

Patience & Tolerance

"**Patience** and **Tolerance** should not be
read as signs of weakness. They are
signs of strength."
— Dalai Lama

<u>PATIENCE</u>

Patience is the capacity to accept or tolerate delay, trouble, or suffering without getting angry or upset.

It is the ability to wait something out or endure difficult circumstances.

The more patient you are,
the more *accepting* you will be of what is, rather than insisting that life be exactly as you would like it to be.

When you practice patience,
you allow yourself the needed time to clearly examine any experience and respond with wisdom rather than react with impatience.

"Patience is the calm acceptance that
things can happen in a different order
than the one you have in mind."
— David G. Allen

Patience adds a dimension of ease and acceptance to your life.

(Please See Chapter 26 Acceptance)

Being impatient will almost always cause you stress...
whereas practicing patience will usually lead to inner peace.

Perhaps the people closest to you are the ones that
try your patience the most...
patience can teach you to respond to them with empathy and
compassion which can only help strengthen your relationships
with them.

Patience is all-important for you to remain faithful
to your commitments to Remain Sober
Maintain a Healthy Lifestyle
Seek Happiness and Contentment

In keeping your commitment to *remain sober*,
your will need to have patience,
because *patience* is about *not giving up* and *not giving in...*
it is the forgoing of unhealthy, short term pleasures for
the far more beneficial long term happiness.

Patience is key to *living in the present.*

It helps you to accept the present moment, just as it is.

Being patient with *yourself* is part of
self-compassion.

(See the section on Self-Compassion in Chapter 10 Healing)

Conscious of humanity, you recognize that no one is perfect...
not even you.

With patience,
you speak to yourself with kindness,
knowing that you're struggling with something,
yet you are confident that you can get through it.

However, if you are impatient with yourself and
judge yourself harshly,
criticizing your progress,
denying yourself your own support, limiting belief in yourself,
you will surely impede your recovery.

By treating yourself with self-compassion and patience,
believing in yourself,
you will strengthen yourself from within and allow yourself
the time it takes to heal and recover.

While the world we live in appears to be impatient and uncaring,
patience helps us to be gentle and forgiving...
not just to others but to ourselves, as well.

Practicing patience, you act from a place of kindness...
friendly, generous and considerate.

Being patient, kind and forgiving to yourself will allow you to
learn from your mistakes and help you to grow in your recovery.

"Have patience with all things, but, first of
all, with yourself."
— St. Francis de Sales

With patience,
you can embrace yourself with self-compassion and self-acceptance,
and focus on your progress,
while being kind to yourself if you are not perfect.

Have Faith in yourself.

Believe in yourself.

Be Patient with yourself.

TOLERANCE

"Tolerance is the positive and cordial
effort to understand another's beliefs,
practices, and habits without
necessarily sharing or accepting them."
— Joseph E. Osborne

Tolerance is the ability or willingness to endure,
acknowledge,
accept or
put up with something,
without interference,
in particular,
the existence of opinions or behaviors that you don't
necessarily agree with.

It is not supporting what you believe is wrong
but showing kindness in spite of your disagreement.

It is the acceptance of the differing views of others...
treating people with fairness who hold these views.

Tolerance is about Kindness and Acceptance.

(Please See Chapter 34 Kindness and Generosity and also
Chapter 26 Acceptance)

Everyone has their own opinions and
values that should be respected and accepted.

As a tolerant person, you understand and accept the
different ideals and beliefs of others
and do not put your opinions above theirs even when you are
certain that you are right.

Tolerance is about *understanding* and *sympathetic awareness.*

It is the acceptance of others as they are and the acceptance
of yourself for who you are.

It promotes a non-judgmental,
open minded and patient attitude
towards difficult experiences and circumstances.

If you practice mindfulness, you will also be practicing tolerance.

(Please See Chapter 25 Mindfulness)

Tolerance is an inner strength...
an integral part of your defense system against life's stresses
and challenges and it is essential to your recovery.

Being tolerant allows you to think more openly and enjoy
greater inner peace.

Tolerance leads to less stress and greater happiness.

Practicing tolerance will allow you to deal more effectively
with persons from various backgrounds,
avoiding unnecessary stress and difficulties,
aiding you in your new happy and sober lifestyle.

"Tolerance is giving to every other human
being every right that you claim for
yourself."
— Robert Green Ingersoll

Happiness, Contentment and Inner Peace

Happiness...Contentment...Inner Peace

Have you ever gone looking for something,
only to realize you had it with you the whole time?

Happiness

"True happiness comes from having a
sense of inner peace and contentment,
which in turn must be achieved by
cultivating altruism, love and
compassion, and by eliminating anger,
selfishness and greed."
— Dalai Lama

Happiness is a positive and joyful state of mind...
a state of well-being...
with feelings of satisfaction and fulfillment...
a sense of enjoyment of and enthusiasm for life.

We all experience
positive and negative emotions (feelings and moods)...

Both positive and negative emotions are crucial for survival.

While the role of most negative emotions is to warn us of dangers
and to keep us safe,
positive emotions are there to help us thrive, progress and
be happy.

Although it is necessary to experience positive and negative emotions,
happiness occurs when the positive outweighs the negative
in the balance scale of emotions...
because positive emotions just make you feel happy.

Although a portion of your happiness has been predetermined by your DNA,
you can still influence your level of happiness to a large degree...
but you must *choose* to take on that responsibility.

If you want to be happy, you can *choose* to change and manage your state of mind.

Happiness is not a blessing that is showered only upon a chosen few...
It's a *choice* given to each one us.

You deserve to be happy...just choose it!

Better yet, *commit* to it...

You owe it to yourself...because...You Are Worth It!

Happiness is a way to experience life and once you have
had a taste of the real life,
a happy and healthy life without the need for alcohol,
you will **never** want to go back to the way it was
when you were drinking.

"Happiness doesn't depend on any
external conditions. It is governed by
your mental attitude."
— Dale Carnegie

True happiness is an inside job...to find it you must look within.

Happiness is a state of mind...
a way of approaching yourself and the world you live in.

It is already within you...
Just trust in your inner wisdom.

Your life will always be filled with challenges...
Recognize that and choose to be happy anyway.

"Who looks outside, dreams.
Who looks inside, awakes."
— Carl Jung

Genuine happiness comes from within and can be cultivated
through mindfulness meditation
and focusing on all the good positive experiences you encounter.

Happiness will come *to you* when it comes *from you.*

It is not about collecting material things or beautiful memories.

It's about having a deep feeling of contentment and
knowing that life is a blessing...Life is a gift.

Happiness will never come to those who fail to appreciate
what they already have.

Although external experiences complement your overall happiness,
internal factors are absolutely *essential* to achieving a life of
joy, happiness and contentment.

Real happiness comes from within and can be developed through
positive thinking, focusing on the good, positive affirmations,
meditation, and mindfulness.

"The greatest discovery of my generation is that human beings
can alter their lives by altering their *attitudes of mind.*"
— William James

While there are many healthy and enjoyable pursuits or activities
that can bring you pleasure,
increasing your overall happiness,
real and lasting happiness is not dependent upon the external world.

Here are some simple ways to increase happiness that are
totally within your control

...Think Less and Feel More
...Frown Less and Smile More
...Talk Less and Listen More.
...Judge Less and Accept More
...Complain Less and Appreciate More
...Fear Less and Love More

Here are some things you should eliminate if you
want to be Happy

...Limiting Beliefs
...Blaming Others
...Negative self-talk
...Dwelling on the past
...Resistance to change
...The need to impress others
...The need to always be right
...The need for other's approval

You need to take a balanced approach and seek happiness
both internally through positive thinking,
mindfulness and meditation...
and also externally through positive strategies and actions.

Keep engaging in your own happiness pursuits...
your commitment to seek happiness and contentment.

It will be worth it!

You are worth it!

The Dalai Lama and Howard Cutler, M.D., in their book,
The Art of Happiness, sum it up this way:

"...one begins by identifying those factors
which lead to happiness and those
which lead to suffering.
Having done this, one then sets about
gradually eliminating those factors which
lead to suffering and
cultivating those which lead to
happiness."

Simply stated: Reduce Your Negativity
Increase Your Positivity

Contentment

Many consider happiness and contentment as being synonymous...
but that's not true...
although they share similarities, they are not exactly the same.

Contentment is an emotional state of satisfaction...
a state of having accepted one's situation...
It is a milder or more tentative form of happiness.

Although they are both positive emotional states
that you can experience,
happiness refers to a state of being happy or feeling good...
contentment refers to a state of being satisfied.

Even the happiest person on earth goes through times
of temporary unhappiness.

However, since contentment is a state of being, it is more enduring,
more permanent, more long lasting than happiness.

But contentment doesn't mean that
you desire nothing...

rather, it is the simple decision to be happy with what you have and patient for what may come.

While happiness denotes an emotional state which is relatively short-term, contentment refers to a state which is more long-term.

Unlike happiness, contentment involves a stable calmness.

Achievement is the source of temporary happiness.

Contentment is the source of lasting happiness.

Unless you also develop contentment,
your happiness may not be sustained...
You cannot have a consistent happy life unless you
learn to be content in all situations.

Cultivating gratitude, thankfulness and appreciation
for what you have
naturally leads to happiness, yet closer to contentment.

Contentment is the calm, quiet, serene
and peaceful side of happiness.

When you are truly content,
you are satisfied and pleased with your situation in life and
are not hoping for any change or improvement.

Contentment is not the fulfillment of
what you want,
but the realization and appreciation of
what you already have.

"Content people don't always have the
best of everything, but they *make* the
best of everything."
— Rachel Cruze

Inner Peace or Peace of Mind

"Do not let the behavior of others destroy
your inner peace."
— Dalai Lama

Inner peace is the state of physical and
spiritual calm, despite having many stressors...
the ability to enjoy peace in each and every moment.

It is a state of emotional poise, confidence
and inner strength...
being confident that no matter what life throws at you,
you will be okay.

Inner peace is more about *being* than *doing.*

As you lose your interest in judging others,
you will start to gain your inner peace.

To find your peace of mind means finding
happiness, contentment and bliss no matter
how difficult things become in your life.

It begins when you choose to not allow
anyone or anything to negatively influence your emotions.

It doesn't mean being in a place where
there is no noise, troubles or difficulties...
it means being in the midst of those things and still
maintaining a calm mind and heart.

When you have *inner peace you*
...stop worrying about everything
...stop obsessing over the past
...forgive yourself and others
...become more at ease with yourself
...do what you love to do

...are honest with yourself
...take things on with a gentle approach
...let life play out on its own.

You can only maintain your inner peace by
living in the present moment.

(Please See Chapter 24 Living in the Present Moment)

Inner peace or peace of mind,
eliminates anxieties, worries and even fears...
removes negative thoughts, stresses and unhappiness.

As it is with happiness and contentment, having an attitude
of gratitude is a prerequisite for inner peace.

"Peace is the result of training your mind
to process life as it is, rather than as you
think it should be."
— Wayne Dyer

Also crucial for peace of mind is the
letting go of and accepting those things you cannot control.

When you become **happy** and **content** and have **inner peace**,
you will, without any doubt, remain true to your
Three Commitments.

Resilience

"The key to life is resilience...We will
always be knocked down. It's the
getting up that counts."
— Dominique Browning

There is not one person alive who is immune from life's problems, challenges and difficulties.

If you think you've already had your share,
Expect More...
It's an inevitable part of living.

The good news is...
With wise preparation, you should be able to survive, recover, work through them and bounce back.

Resilience is the capacity to recover quickly from problematic situations...
the ability to become strong or healthy again after something bad happens.

It's the capacity to withstand adversity and rebound from difficult life events.

Being resilient doesn't mean that you don't experience adversity and misfortune...
It doesn't mean you don't feel stress, suffering or emotional upheaval.

It means that you are able to work through the emotional pain and suffering...

able to cope with living in the midst of stresses...
recover from stressful situations in the face of adversity...
overcome life's challenges and work through your problems.

"Life is not the way it's supposed to be...
It's the way it is...The way we cope with
it, is what makes the difference."
— Unknown

Part of resiliency is the capacity to cope.

Coping is the ability to face and deal with
responsibilities, problems and difficulties,
in a calm and peaceful manner.

Keep in mind that tough times never last...but *tough people do.*

Resiliency is your ability to adapt and have tolerance,
when things don't go as planned....
not dwelling on failures...
learning from your mistakes and then moving forward...
focusing your time and energy on changing the things
that you have control over...
accepting the things that cannot be changed.

Having resilience is what enables you to adapt well to or recover
from adversity, trauma, tragedy, threats and stresses...
which is absolutely essential to your recovery.

Resilience is an all-important trait to
possess if your goal is to be happy and content.

Positive emotions partially exist to help you recover from
the ill effects of damaging negative emotions.

Cultivating more positivity can help you become more resilient
in the face of a crisis, trauma or stressful situations.

Your goal should be to let your positive emotions
outnumber the negative.

When you feel more positive emotions than negative ones,
difficult situations become easier to tackle.

Positive emotions build your resilience...
the emotional resources you will need for coping.

They broaden your awareness and let you
see more options for problem solving.

"Resilience is knowing that ***you*** are the
only person who has the power and the
responsibility to pick yourself up."
— Mary Holloway

WAYS IN WHICH TO BUILD RESILIENCE:

*Learn to relax through *self care* and
meditation and by not taking everything
in your life, so seriously.

*Learn from your mistakes and failures...
looking back on what was helpful in
previous times of difficulties, you can
re-evaluate and make any
necessary positive changes.

*Choose your responses...responding
calmly and logically to take control and
find a solution.

*Maintain a Hopeful Outlook - it's hard
to be positive when things don't go
your way...

An optimistic outlook can
help you to expect that everything
will work out...
anticipating positive results.

*Build *Self-empowerment* - this will give
you the courage and strength you
need to move forward through life's
difficulties and challenges.

*Be Flexible - carefully made plans may
need to be amended or scrapped...
acccpt situations you cannot change.

Being resilient means you need to be
committed to your own well-being...to be your own protector...
someone who will look out for you...
to recognize that you have rights and that you matter.

Resilience involves more than just
surviving through and bouncing back from life's challenges.

It's having the capacity to pursue opportunities
despite having difficulties and facing challenges...
the ability to go on, day after day...
with the motivation and determination to continue to
pursue your goals...remembering, in your case,
your Three Commitments of

remaining sober...
maintaining your new sober lifestyle...
being happy and content.

Gratitude... a direct line to happiness and contentment

"Gratitude unlocks the fullness of life. It
turns what we have into enough, and
more. It turns denial into acceptance,
chaos to order, confusion to clarity.
It turns a meal into a feast, a house into
a home, a stranger into a friend.
Gratitude makes sense of our past,
brings peace for today and creates a
vision for tomorrow."
— Melody Beattie

Gratitude is...
the quality of being thankful...
the readiness to show appreciation for and to return kindness...
acknowledging the *goodness* in your life.

(Please See Chapter 34 Kindness and Generosity)

It is having appreciation...

appreciating your life as it is right now...
looking at the brighter side of a situation...
savoring life's positive experiences...
taking pleasure in the gifts that you've been given...
counting all your blessings...

feeling enjoyment and satisfaction from your current
circumstances and not taking things for granted.

Being grateful for your life and
all the good in it, will definitely make you a happier person.

Gratitude naturally leads to happiness.

"If you want to find happiness, find
gratitude."
— Steve Maraboli

Gratefulness is a tremendous source of happiness.

It unlocks the richness of life and turns what you already have
into *enough*...a satisfying feeling of contentment.

When you are grateful and appreciative of what you have
in your life,
not overly concerned with what you are lacking,
you will naturally find peace, contentment and happiness
from within.

"Acknowledging the good that you already
have in your life is the foundation for
abundance."
— Eckhart Tolle

You can begin to cultivate gratitude by finding joy in the little things...
the smile from a friend...
the kindness of a stranger...
the beauty of a sunset.

Savor...Absorb...and Pay Special Attention to the Good.

There will always be something that you want or think you need...
but if your main focus is on obtaining more and more,
you will never appreciate and enjoy what you already have.

Gratitude is having that appreciation and enjoyment.

If you want to be happy, you need to change the emphasis of your thinking from what you want, to what you have.

Your happiness does not depend on getting the next thing
you think you need, in your life.

So how DOES gratitude make you happy?

To begin with, *gratitude* is the antidote for most negative emotions...
a neutralizer of envy, jealousy, greed, hostility, worry
and irritation.

You will continue to have the stress and challenges
that are part of life...
having gratitude will help you to cope with life's problems.

The appreciation of your current circumstances help you cope
by reinterpreting your stressful or negative life experiences
in a positive way.

You have and you will continue to have disappointments
and misfortunes in your life.

These can be quite challenging to your recovery.

How will you react to these upsets?

By practicing gratitude,
being thankful and focusing your attention on the good,
you will help create positive thoughts and feelings,
leading to a contented and happy state of mind.

This happy mental state is an inner strength,
a defense against hard times...
serving as a protection against life's challenges and difficulties.

"The struggle ends when gratitude begins."
— Neale Donald Walsch

By relishing and taking in the little joys in your life,
you'll be able to extract the most satisfaction from
your circumstances.

Being consciously aware or mindful of what you are thankful for
can increase your level of awareness.

Each morning, when you open your eyes, feel grateful for
another day of life.

And at the end of each day,
think on all the positive things that you experienced throughout
the day and be thankful for them.

Being grateful for your life and all the good in it,
will most surely lead to happiness.

Having gratitude you will experience many positive emotions,
such as joy, pride and interest, and
less negative emotions, like anger, sadness and anxiety.

Having more positive and less negative emotions can
only lead to an increase in your overall happiness.

Notice all the good things that people do for you and
thank them for it.

It really doesn't require much effort...
Just a simple "Thank You!"

Notice good things throughout your day and make a point
to store them in your mind...
This will help you to remember all the positive things
you can appreciate...
There's no need to take note of the negative experiences...
your negatively biased brain will not easily let you forget them.

Having gratitude will not only increase your positive emotions...
It will help you to thoroughly enjoy good experiences.
It will help you to face life's challenges, maintain
good relationships,
all of which will make for a happier you.

When you thank someone and really mean it, doesn't it
make you feel good?

The more you express thanks or feel gratitude,
the less time, the less room you will have for negative thoughts
and emotions.

The more you practice and express gratitude,
the stronger your self-worth and
self-confidence will grow.

It will help you to have less negativity overall.

Yes, *less* negativity...
You will always have some, but your super-inner-strength of
gratitude will give you the stability you need to deal with it.

Gratitude is also a very *giving* state of mind, which makes
you feel good,
whether you are expressing gratitude or receiving it from someone.

How could it not? It's all positive and constructive.

Of course, you will always have some negative thoughts and emotions...
but with an attitude of gratitude, you will not have to
waste your energy trying to fight them...
You can just let them be.

When you are grateful, everything in your life becomes:

more Beautiful
more Delicious
more Wonderful
more Brilliant
more Amazing
more Enjoyable
more Satisfying

What you already Have, becomes *Enough!*

There are almost an infinite amount of things to be grateful for.

There are so many things you are most likely grateful for that you just may not usually consider but by acknowledging them and bringing your attention to them, it will most assuredly increase your positivity which, in turn, will boost your happiness.

Some things to be grateful for:

Your Recovery
Your Health
Your Five Senses
Smiles
Compliments from Strangers
The Kindness of Others
Your Home
Your Friends and Family
Sunshine
Modern Medicine
Our Beautiful Planet
Education
Clean Water
Sunday mornings and weekends
A Good Book
Your favorite foods

Alone Time
The Changing Seasons
Honesty
Your Pets
Hearing a child laugh
Your unique personality
Your creativity
Your sense of humor
Your accomplishments
Holding hands for the first time
First Kisses
Being in Love or Loving someone
Having someone you can Trust
Laughter
A Hug...getting or giving
Gifts...to you or from you
Intimacy
Having a Job
Your cell phone
Taking a hot shower
Having a soft, warm bed
A quiet place to sit and think
Flowers...giving or getting
Photos
The view out your window
Your morning coffee
Sleeping In
Waking up an hour before your alarm
Morning walks
The Sound of Birds Singing
Beautiful Sunrises and Sunsets
Listening to and Feeling the Wind
Shooting Stars
Meditation (at any time of day)
A Moonlit Night
The Breathtaking View of the Stars
Climbing into Bed
A Goodnight Kiss

Falling Asleep Tired and Satisfied
Farmers
Service workers
Nature and marked hiking trails
Toilet paper (what was it like before?)
Art and Art museums
Your favorite Music...live or recorded
Diversity
Holidays...all of them
Vaccines
Happy Memories
Rainy days
Teachers
Passing a Test
Campfires
Rainbows
Snow
Picnics
Birthdays
Support groups
Sports
Vacations
Netflix
Hearing your favorite Song on the radio
A Meal with those you love
Get Togethers
Fresh Baked Cookies
Tea before Bed
Pizza and Movie Night
Fridays

And there's probably hundreds, if not thousands more.

Life can be a challenge and can, at times, be cruel, but there is also so, so much that we can be grateful for.

And having an attitude of gratitude will help you to remain faithful to your three commitments...

to remain sober...
to maintain your healthy lifestyle...
to seek happiness and contentment

Kindness and Generosity

Kindness

"Kindness is the language which the deaf
can hear and the blind can see."
— Mark Twain

In a world where you can do anything, Be Kind!

Kindness is the quality of being
friendly,
generous,
considerate,
gentle,
warm and affectionate.

Being kind is doing intentional, voluntary acts of kindness,
not only when it's easy or convenient but also
when it's difficult and inconvenient.

It is your ability to accept people and situations for what they are,
without hating them or getting caught up in what you
don't like about them.

Kindness *costs nothing* but *means everything.*

While kindness has a connotation of weakness,
being kind actually requires courage and strength.

Being **nice** is when you are polite to people and treat them well.

Being **kind** is when you care about people and show you care.

"You cannot do a kindness too soon, for
you never know how soon it will be too late."
— Ralph Waldo Emerson

Kindness is being openly happy for another person...
a willingness to celebrate their successes.

An act of kindness can produce feelings of self-confidence and
being in control of your life...
which is extremely important for your recovery.

Developing kindness is one way that will help you to deal
with conditions you may not be able to change.

There are and will always be people in need...
Can you find it in your heart to extend kindness and lend
a helping hand?

Kindness is a gift everyone can afford to give.

You will never regret being kind!

If you have the chance to make people happy, just do it...
do it for others...do it for yourself...
Just Do It !!!

Sometimes people are struggling silently...
Maybe, your act of kindness can make their day.

Kindness, not unlike love, is being selfless, caring,
compassionate and unconditionally kind.

If we could all remember that none of us are perfect,
we would be a lot kinder to each other and to ourselves.

Kindness is a positive quality,
an inner strength,
a type of behavior marked by acts of compassion,
concern, courtesy, friendliness, gentleness, helpfulness,

patience, sympathy, tenderness, thoughtfulness,
tolerance, understanding and unselfishness.

When we practice kindness either to other people or
towards ourselves,
we can experience positive mental and physical changes...
lowering stress levels, and
increasing the body's production of feel-good hormones
such as dopamine, oxytocin and serotonin.

There are so many ways in which you could practice kindness...
these are just a few:

Volunteer your time to a local organization

Give a smile or a compliment to a stranger

Donate to a charitable foundation

Hold the door for someone

Work at a homeless shelter

Bring donuts to friends or co-workers, nurses at a hospital or
first responders at a police or fire station

Help someone cross the street or carry their groceries

Water or mow your neighbor's lawn

People who participate in acts of kindness have been shown to
increase their self-worth, empathy and compassion,
and improve their mood.

Practice kindness...being kind will help you to be emotionally
healthier and aid you in staying faithful to your commitments.

"In the end, *only kindness matters.*"
— Jewel

Generosity

"No one can sincerely try to help another
without helping themselves."
— Charles D. Warner

Generosity is the act of being kind, selfless and giving to others...
although the act of giving is done to benefit others,
it will paradoxically increase your own well-being and mental health.

True generosity is an offering...
given freely and out of pure love...no strings attached.

"No one has ever become poor by giving."
— Anne Frank

Many people live in fear and hold on tightly to what they have
because they do not trust that there will be more.

The best way to overcome your fear of not having enough
is through generosity.

Giving is a fearless act that will reward you by bringing you joy.

Generosity can make you healthier and happier...
When you do something good for another person,
you encourage the release of endorphins (*feel good chemicals*)
in your body which brings about a 'helper's high'
and helps fight against stress...

It just makes you feel good and feeling good will
ultimately increase your happiness.

Both kindness and generosity are wonderful qualities...
they encourage you to express heartfelt interest in
the welfare of others.

At the same time, generous and kind acts can give you comfort,
satisfaction and feelings of contentment.

"Attention is the rarest and purest form of
generosity."
— Simone Weil

Your time and your love are two of the most valuable possessions
that you can share.

It has long been recognized that
carrying out acts of kindness and generosity raise levels
of happiness and well-being...
a connection between the performance of selfless acts and
feelings of happiness and contentment.

By your acts of kindness and generosity, you may experience
a pleasant feeling,
known in behavioral studies as a *warm glow*...
It's built into your neurochemistry...doing good leads to feeling good.

A Loving-Kindness Meditation

"Be kinder to yourself...And then let
your kindness flood the world."
— Pema Chödrön

Loving-Kindness is tenderness and consideration towards
yourself and others...
tender kindness, motivated by affection...
the type of kindness which is based on or arises from love.

Loving-Kindness meditation is a self-care strategy
that can help reduce your stress...
increase your sense of well-being...
your capacity for forgiveness...
your connection to all humanity.

It's about sending out benevolent and loving thoughts or kind
intentions to yourself, your loved ones, your neighbors, and
to all humankind,
including those with whom you may have
had disagreements or conflicts.

The following is a basic, yet effective example of a loving-kindness
meditation you may want to try...

Find a comfortable spot...seated or lying down.

Close your eyes and relax your body, from your head to your feet.

Start by taking three or four deep breaths.

Allow yourself to feel a sense of emotional well-being and
inner peace...
having complete love and gratitude for all that you are.

Reflect on your desire for peace,
happiness and
freedom
from suffering.

Repeat the following phrases to yourself:

May I Be Happy

May I Be At Ease

May I Be Free From Suffering

Feel the love and kindness of these phrases...
the feelings of warmth and contentment.

Acknowledge your wish to be happy, at peace, safe and protected.

Speak these phrases to yourself in a kind and friendly manner.

You may wish to repeat these phrases over and over,
as a statement of your benevolent intentions.

As you become more comfortable receiving the kindness of
these phrases, begin to add others into your practice.

Start with someone you are already connected to...
perhaps your child, a parent, your spouse or a good friend.

Extend your gratitude and love as you direct these phrases
towards them...

May You Be Happy

May You Be At Ease

May You Be Free From Suffering

After extending these feelings towards that person for a while,
begin to include others into your awareness...
other family members, friends and acquaintances.

May You As Well Be Happy

May You Also Be At Ease

May You Too Be Free From Suffering

Finally, after some time,
try sending out feelings of love and kindness to all of humanity...
focusing on connecting to all beings throughout the world...
even those with beliefs and ideologies to which you are opposed.

May You All Be Happy

May You All Be At Ease

May You All Be Free From Suffering

When you decide to end your meditation,
gently open your eyes and take a few deep breaths.

Try to internalize how this meditation of loving-kindness
makes you feel.

Try to recall these feelings throughout the remainder of your day.

The main goal of this type of meditation is to develop
unconditional positive emotions toward all beings...
including feelings of love, joy, gratitude,
happiness, forgiveness, compassion and connection.

"When we feel love and kindness towards
others, it helps us all develop inner
happiness and peace."
— The Dalai Lama

CHAPTER 36

My Self-Improvement Journey

"Become addicted to constant and
never-ending self-improvement."
— Anthony J. D'Angelo

Everyday most people throughout the world share one hope –
to improve their lives.

It all happens with learning something new.

My self-help journey began with reading personal-development
or self-improvement books.

They were to me, the biggest and most enjoyable part of my recovery.

I'm convinced that they are what inspired me to write this book...
In fact, writing this book was part of what aided me in my recovery.

I utilized these inspiring resources every single day.

The knowledge and wisdom I gained, helped me to feel empowered
and in control of my life.

My goal was to learn to be the best possible version of myself.

Through the education I gained from reading and studying these
publications, I was able to improve my thinking and understanding
and to adjust my attitude,
my outlook,
my entire life.

The comprehension I gained, helped me to center my attention on what mattered to me...
to achieve my goals and keep my commitments, expand my awareness and ultimately increase my happiness.

It's all about personal growth and improving your emotional health.

It's a lifelong educational journey that never ends.

Self-help and Self-improvement books will inspire you with *positivities* and *possibilities.*

They will encourage you take the necessary steps to better yourself
...to make the changes you need to make
...to realize that you can be more than what or who you are.

The information and wisdom from these resources can motivate you to improve...
to help you to see things from a new perspective...
to interpret life in a different way...
to enable you to see what is possible...
to help you break through your self imposed limitations.

Reading and learning something new and positive every day
is a sure way to improve your life.

But Self-Help and Self-Improvement publications can do more than just help you improve yourself
... they encourage you to develop a curious attitude
... expand your current knowledge
... create in you a hunger for growth and excellence
... instill in you a desire for continued learning.

These inspiring books do more than just improve your life
...they enhance your life.

They prompt you to take an honest evaluation of your life choices
while helping you appreciate the changes you need to make.

Almost immediately after I stopped drinking alcohol,
while beginning my recovery from my
Alcohol Use Disorder,
I started to read books that would help me to be a better person
as well as a happier one.

In that year of recovery, I read so many books on various subjects,
the majority of them, self- improvement books.

More than just *read* these books,
I studied them as you would a text book
...reading and re-reading,
highlighting points I thought applied to me,
making pages and pages of notes.

Learning doesn't end after you're finished
with school...your education is never completed.

"The capacity to learn is a gift...The ability
to learn is a skill...The willingness to learn
is a choice."
— Brian Herbert

The more you learn, the more equipped you become to
accomplish your goals and stay faithful to your commitments —
remaining sober, maintaining your new lifestyle and
becoming happier and more content.

I have read books on

...Happiness
...Staying Sober
...Meditation
...Cognitive Behavioral Therapy
...Kindness

...Buddhist Principles
...Self-Compassion
...Mindfulness
...Positive Psychology
...Neuropsychology and Neuroscience.

I also read hundreds of articles and research papers on these subjects and many more.

The top ten books I believe to be most important for your self-improvement are:

1 "The Art of Happiness" by Dr Howard Cutler and The Dalai Lama

2 "The Everything Guide to Cognitive Behavioral Therapy" Ellen Bowers, PhD

3 "Don't Sweat the Small Stuff" R.Carlson

4 "The How of Happiness" S.Lyubomirsky

5 "Real Happiness" S.Salzberg

6 "Stillness Speaks" E.Tolle

7 "The Sober Truth" L.Dodes M.D

8 "The Four Agreements" D.M.Ruiz

9 "Hardwiring Happiness" R.Hanson, PhD

10 "Voices of Insight" S.Salzberg

It has been said that self-improvement takes a long time.

And while that is true,
even before finishing my first book,
I began to reap some significant benefits...
taking in the insightful information and positive strategies...
instantly applying them to my life.

In a sense, my self-improvement began almost immediately.

Be patient and recognize that change can take time and
it usually comes in small increments.

Enjoy the process of gradually letting go of your negativity and
increasing your positivity.

It's a journey of learning...
of healing and recovering...
of personal growth and positive change.

Celebrate your victories!!!

It's a great feeling to know that YOU are responsible for your
personal growth, for the positive changes in your life.

I continue to read, study and learn from self-help and self-improvement
books and I really don't see myself ever stopping.

I enjoy seeing and feeling my own personal growth
...gradually seeing more and more positive changes in my life
...increasing my happiness and overall feeling of contentment.

I encourage you to start your own self-help/self-improvement journey.

Become committed to your personal growth and recovery
...with the goal of becoming a better version of yourself.

Just remember to be patient...
everyone is a beginner at some point...
It's a gradual learning process.

“Education breeds confidence.
Confidence breeds hope.
Hope breeds peace.”
— Confucius

Never stop learning because life never stops teaching!

The Benefits of Exercise

"You are only one workout away from a good mood."
Unknown

Exercise in any way, shape or form
will contribute to your happiness.

The more your body is in motion, the less your mind is bombarded
with insignificant thoughts.

It can give your mind an emotional break as well as
a feeling of accomplishment.

Physical activity reduces anxiety and stress...
increases your quality of life...
improves your sleep and protects against cognitive impairment.

When you exercise,
not only do you feel good that you're accomplishing something,
you also experience the benefits of improved physical fitness.

Exercise...seriously, **go exercise...**
your body and mind will thank you for it.

When you move around during your exercise session,
your body is just doing what it was meant to do.

Exercise releases Endorphins for pain relief, Serotonin -
a mood stabilizer and Norepinephrine...
These increase happiness levels...
lower stress levels and help reduce anxiety.

This is especially important to your recovery.

Exercise should absolutely be a part of your self-care routine.

It improves your overall health and can help repair some of the damage you've done to your body processes and brain functions from your excessive drinking of alcohol.

Exercise will promote

...positive changes in your brain
...reduced inflammation
...more confident attitude
...new neural growth
...feelings of calm and relaxation
...better sleep

Working out also encourages the production of chemicals that prevent degeneration of your hippocampus,
the part of your brain involved in learning and memory.

The type of exercise doesn't matter, whether it's aerobic (walking, running, swimming) or anaerobic (strength training).

If you can do both, so much the better.

Strength training can lead to a significant increase in your sense of confidence which is also important to your recovery.

I personally try for five days a week of working out with dumbbells.
It's hard work but it's so worth it...
When you take of your body, your body responds in kind.

Of course, one of the best types of exercise is hiking in nature...
It refreshes both your body and your mind..

(Please see Chapter 38 Nature and Hiking).

Exercise can also help you control or maintain your weight...
improve your mood and boost your energy level...
strengthens your immune system and combats
health conditions and diseases.

Exercise is for everyone...it's never too late to start.

And exercise is just plain fun...
well, maybe not fun,
but you have got to love the after effects.

The best feeling is when you didn't want to exercise and
you worked out anyway...
I never regret it when I do but I always regret it when I don't.

Nature and Hiking in Nature

Nature

"Take a course in good water and air,
in the eternal youth of nature, may you
renew your own.
Go quietly, alone, no harm will befall
you."
— John Muir

Fresh air, sun, plants, trees and wildlife...*The beauty of nature.*

Being outdoors in nature can be healing and beneficial for both your body and mind.

Breathe in the fresh air,
soak up the rays from the sun, and
feel renewed...
feel wonderful.

Take in the vast array of vibrant colors.

Listen to the calming sounds of nature...the babbling of a brook, the rustling of leaves or a sweet melody from the birds.

Smell the fragrances of the land, the air and the water.

Nature can help you disconnect from your daily stresses by engaging your senses and quieting your mind...
it just feels so natural or organic.

And nature has such strong healing properties...

...improving your mind
...boosting your immune system
...increasing your positivity

Nature can take you out of the prison of
your mind...
where you can be lost in overthinking, remembering/ruminating
or anxiously anticipating...
lost in a complexed maze of self-centered problems and
help you stay focused in the present moment.

Nature can generate in you a number of positive emotions such as
calmness, joy,
awe, wonder,
satisfaction and contentment.

Looking around at the boundless beauty
of nature just naturally causes you to be happy.

Give yourself completely to the subtle sounds, sights and smells
of nature...
It's as if they all exist for your delight...
Actually, They Do!!!

In Japan, they have a poetic term to refer to spending time in
the woods...
they call it shinrin-yoku -
"forest bathing" or "taking in the forest atmosphere".

Go to the "atmosphere" of the forest
and soak it all in...
Immerse yourself in a luxuriously sweet bath of nature.

Spending time in nature reduces stress and calms anxiety.

It opens your senses to your surroundings and
improves your sensory perception.

Just being surrounded by nature will help keep you *in the present*, with feelings of calm and peace as well as awe and amazement.

Hiking in Nature

"You're off to great places,
today is your day.
Your mountain is waiting,
so get on your way."
- Dr. Seuss

The combination of nature and hiking can increase both your physical and emotional health.

Hiking is one of the best ways to get exercise...
It's a great *whole-body* workout.

Hiking helps build stronger muscles and bones as well as your cardiovascular system...
and it improves your overall physical balance.

In addition to the physical benefits of hiking in nature,
it also helps to keep your mind in the present and evokes in you
a sense of calmness, tranquility and serenity.

It has the ability to reduce stress,
stabilize your mood and
decompress your mind so that your body and mind are both able to relax.

Especially when you are hiking on a new or unknown trail,
will you need all of your senses,
your entire body as well as your brain,
to navigate the unpredictable obstacles you will encounter...
tree roots, slippery rocks, overhanging branches and forest wildlife.

It's wondrous to see and feel your body and mind working in perfect harmony.

As you are trekking through the trails,
your brain and body work together,
to make immediate decisions and adjustments for your protection.

This form of physical activity induces the release of endorphins...
a powerful chemical in your brain,
which energizes you and
makes you happier.

Just being in nature is very calming...
and when you're trudging through the woods you can't help but
remain in the present,
where your problems take a back seat.

Being in nature encourages feelings of *awe*,
a powerful, positive emotion,
which fills you with wonder and happiness.

Hiking is a way for nature to give both your body and mind
some much needed therapy...
helping you to disconnect from all
the pressures and challenges of everyday life.

As you breathe, smell, touch, see and listen to the wilderness,
all else seems to fade away.

You Feel Alive...
tired and fatigued and yet so refreshed and relaxed.

If you've ever gone hiking, you know what an incredible and
rewarding workout it can be.

Participating in this intense exercise in nature, provides
so many benefits for

...your brain
...your mind
...your senses
...your entire body

"Nature itself is the best physician."
— Hippocrates

My wife and I usually hike in the various forests of New England, especially those with waterfalls and streaming rivers.
I like to capture some of the essence of nature with my camera and share the pics with friends and family.

It has become one of the highlights of our week.

And, it's a regular part of my new sober lifestyle...
helping me to stay faithful to my three commitments:
To remain sober
To maintain my healthy lifestyle
To pursue happiness and contentment

Hiking in nature encourages you to *slow down* and *be present* in the natural world.

On your hike, whenever it feels right...
stop...
find a place to sit...
take a few slow and deep breaths...
let go of everything that is not there
in the present moment.

You'll be in the perfect place for meditation...while walking or when you stop to rest.

"Nature does not hurry, yet everything
is accomplished."
— Lao Tzu

CHAPTER 39

Smiling and Laughing

Smiling

♫ "Smile, what's the use of crying?
You'll find that life is still worthwhile,
if you just smile." ♫
— Nat King Cole

Smiling makes you look good and feel marvelous...
It can immediately change your mood...
reduce your stress and anxiety and
help you to stay positive.

It usually happens as an involuntary response to something that
is bringing you joy or laughter, OR
It can also be a totally conscious, intentional choice.

And, as intelligent as you may be,
your brain cannot distinguish the difference between the two
and will respond to either in the exact same way.

It can have an immediate positive effect on your mood,
even reducing any anxiety you may be having.

Putting a smile on your face,
with or without any feelings of joy or happiness,
will trigger the release of dopamine and serotonin
(neurotransmitters),
which can help improve the way you're feeling.

So, next time you're feeling low,
put on a happy facial expression, also known as a smile and
fool your brain into a happy emotional state.

When you become stressed, overwhelmed
or just tired and worn down,
slap on a smile and see what happens.

Reasons to Smile Every Day

Smiling Relieves Stress
Elevates Your Mood
Boosts Your Immune System
May Lower Your Blood Pressure
Reduces Pain
Helps You Look More Attractive
Encourages You To Be Positive

Have you tried it yet?

Humor

Humor is the ability of something or someone, to cause
amusement or laughter...
It is also your ability to find amusement or comedy in something
seen, heard or thought about...
usually causing you to smile and laugh.

Humor is something that is funny, comical,
or amusing...
It can be found in movies, books, jokes and in everyday life...
Laughter is good for you, especially in your recovery,
where adjusting to a new lifestyle can create some challenges.

Laughter

"Laughter is a tranquilizer with
no side effects."
— Arnold Glasow

Life is better when you are laughing...
And if you're too busy to laugh, then you're just way too busy.

Laughter *really is* the best medicine.

So, always laugh when you can...
it won't cost a thing.

Nothing works faster than laughter to bring your mind and body back into balance...
It can lighten your burdens, inspire hope and keep you grounded and focused...
It can help to release any anger or tension you may have as well as encourage you to forgive.

During your recovery process,
it can be a tremendous resource,
an inner strength,
to help surmount problems, challenges and difficulties.

The following is a list of some of the *benefits of laughter* —

PHYSICAL HEALTH BENEFITS

* Boosts Your Immunity
* Lowers Your Stress Hormones
* Decreases Your Pain
* Relaxes Your Muscles

EMOTIONAL HEALTH BENEFITS

* Adds Joy and Zest to Your Life
* Eases Your Anxiety and Tension
* Relieves Your Stress
* Improves Your Mood
* Strengthens Your Resilience

SOCIAL BENEFITS

*Attracts Others to You
*Strengthens Your Relationships
*Enhances Teamwork

In even your darkest hours, if you find something funny,
give yourself permission to laugh.

Laughter is *always right and appropriate...*
unless it is at someone else's expense.

"The most wasted of all days
are the ones without laughter."
— e.e. Cummings

Life is too important to be taken seriously.

Instead of complaining about some of life's problems,
try to laugh at them.

Approaching life in that way,
you may find yourself less stressed about negative situations.

Some ways to create more laughter in your life:

*Set aside some time, every day for
something fun or funny.

*Make a list of various things that make
you smile or laugh.

*Watch standup comics on You Tube
or Netflix.

*Listen to humorous podcasts.

Take yourself a little less seriously and
make a point of laughing at yourself.

Laughter provides both a physical and emotional release...
it brings the focus away from anger, guilt, stress and
negative emotions in a more beneficial way than a mere distraction.

More than just a rescue from sadness, laughter can help you keep
a positive, optimistic attitude,
even through difficult and disappointing experiences.

♫ "If you smile through your fear and
sorrow...Smile and maybe tomorrow
You'll see the sun come shining through for you." ♫
— Nat King Cole

CHAPTER 40

A Summary for You

From the pages of this book you have learned that
Yes, an Awesome Sober Lifestyle is Possible...
that you most certainly can make a
Full Recovery from your Alcohol Use Disorder...
that **you have the power** to make that happen...

but *ONLY* if you are willing to take
Complete Responsibility for Your Life...
accepting the fact that YOU are the cause
and solution of the matter...
answering for your own actions...
being accountable for the choices you make.

Becoming fully responsible for your life,
empowered you to take control of your life...
to make positive choices and positive changes...
to take charge of your destiny...
to begin the healing process...
to learn and put into practice various
approaches to help you remain faithful to your
Three Commitments –

1) To Remain Sober
2) To Maintain a Healthy Lifestyle
3) To Seek Happiness and Contentment

After we considered a number of things
necessary to your early sobriety...
managing stress, dealing with cravings,
and the importance of your support team,
we discussed four main strategies to help you
stay loyal to your Three Commitments.

All four have the same objective...
to Increase the Positivity and Decrease
the Negativity in your life.

One of the four approaches focuses on
Living your Life in The Present Moment.

Living in the Present means that you are aware of
what is happening at this very moment,
focused on or centered in the 'here and now'...
the only place where life happens...
Not *Overthinking...*
dwelling on things from your past that have already passed
and can never be changed or
anxiously worrying about something that
may or may not happen in the future.

Living in the Present is about being *Mindful...*
fully aware of where you are and what you are doing...
not overreacting...
not judging...
not overwhelmed by what's going on around you.

You learned to practice being mindful with
Mindfulness Meditation...
which has as its goal - to achieve a state of alertness...
being intensely aware of what you are experiencing
in the moment without any interpretation or judgment.

Mindfulness is about *Acceptance...*recognizing the reality that
some things cannot be changed...
knowing that resisting or rejecting may cause you
unnecessary suffering.
Accept life as it is, rather than insisting that it be exactly
as you would like it to be.

Letting Go is also a part of Living in the Present...
Let go of the way that you think life should be...
Let go of all the negativity from your past.

When you are Living in the Present Moment, you need to practice *Forgiveness...*

Forgive others, not because they deserve
to be forgiven but because you need to close the door
to the negativity of your past.
Forgive yourself for all the bad decisions you've made...
for your impulsive reactions and behaviors...
the choices you made that caused harm, to others
and to yourself.

When Living in the Present, you need to
have *Patience...*
the capacity to accept or tolerate delay, trouble, or
suffering without getting angry or upset...
The more patient you are, the more *accepting* you will be
of *what is,*
rather than insisting that life be exactly as you would
like it to be.

Slowing Down is also part of Living in the Present Moment...
It makes you more aware of your surroundings...
to see where you are and what is happening...
to be aware of what really matters.

Living in the Present Moment encourages you to *savor* or
attend to and appreciate the positive experiences
of your life.

To a large extent, your happiness, contentment and
peace of mind are based on your ability to
Live in the Present Moment.

Another valuable approach that can ensure your success
in remaining true to your three commitments is to
concentrate primarily on your *Positive Qualities.*

Positive qualities are your personal attributes,
good character traits or inner strengths...
they serve as a protection to your well-being.

Cultivating positive qualities leads to experiencing
positive emotions.

Acts of *Kindness and Generosity* produce feelings of
self-confidence, being in control of your life and
help you to deal with conditions you may not be
able to change...
they encourage you to express heartfelt interest in the
welfare of others...
At the same time, generous and kind acts can give you
comfort, satisfaction and feelings of contentment.

Gratitude is a tremendous source of happiness...
it unlocks the richness of life and turns what you already
have into enough...
a satisfying feeling of contentment.

When you are grateful and appreciative of what you have
in your life,
not overly concerned with what you are lacking,
you will naturally find peace, contentment and happiness
from within.

Having *Resilience* is your ability to adapt
when things don't go as planned....
not dwelling on failures...
learning from your mistakes and then moving forward...
focusing your time and energy on changing the things that
you have control over...
accepting the things that cannot be changed.

Training Your Brain towards positivity is
another approach that will help you to stay faithful
to your commitments.

You have the power to change your brain...
to *train* your brain through self directed positive
neural plasticity.

You can change your brain by training your brain with
Positive Thinking.

By repeating *Positive Affirmations,* practicing
Meditation and *Savoring* your daily positive experiences,
you will strengthen your brain's new neural pathways,
which can transform your new thought patterns,
creating more *Positive Emotions,*
maintaining a more positive state of mind...
leading to an increase of happiness and contentment.

The fourth approach is based on the
Happiness strategies of *Self-Care.*

Self-Care is the practice of taking action to preserve
or improve one's own health...
taking an active role in protecting one's own well-being
and happiness.

Taking good care of yourself helps you to feel good
and feeling good is the foundation of happiness and
contentment.

Exercise, in any shape or form, will contribute to
your happiness.

The more your body is in motion, the less your mind is
bombarded with insignificant thoughts...
giving your mind an emotional break...
reducing anxiety and stress...increasing your quality of life.

Nature can help you disconnect from your daily stresses
by engaging your senses and quieting your mind...
It can take you out of the prison of your mind...

where you can be lost in overthinking,
remembering/ruminating or anxiously anticipating...
lost in a complexed maze of self-centered problems and
it can help you stay focused in the present moment.

In addition to the physical benefits of *Hiking In Nature,*
it also helps to keep your mind in the present and
evokes in you a sense of calmness, tranquility and serenity.

All four approaches,
Learning to Live in the Present,
Focusing on Positive Qualities,
Training your Brain towards Positivity and
Self-Care Strategies,
delivered positive results for me and
I hope they did for you as well.

Please continue to practice these strategies as you
remain on your path of happiness and contentment.

Feel good about your progress and your
determination to stay faithful to your commitments.

Celebrate your Achievements and
do something special for yourself...
something positive that makes you feel good.

It is my wish that, despite any challenges and difficulties
you will encounter,
you continue to persevere with your new,
awesome, healthy and sober lifestyle.

CHAPTER 41

The ABC's of a Continued Happy and Sober Life

Acceptance is a willingness to tolerate a difficult situation...recognizing the reality that some things cannot be changed...
knowing that by resisting or rejecting,
it may cause you unnecessary suffering.
Accept life as it is, rather than insisting that it be exactly as you would like it to be.

(Please See Chapter 26 Acceptance)

Affirmations are positive statements you repeat over and over, to yourself, that can help to challenge and overcome self-sabotaging and negative thinking.
By repeatedly stating these affirmations,
you can rewire or train your brain to think positively.

(Please See Chapter 14 Positive Affirmations)

Alcohol is a colorless, volatile, flammable liquid that is produced by the natural fermentation of sugars and is the intoxicating constituent of wine, beer, spirits, and other drinks.
It is also used as an industrial solvent and as fuel...
a carcinogenic neurotoxin (poison), that can have devastating effects on your brain cells.

Antidote to an unhealthy, destructive emotion - a positive, constructive emotion, realistic, grounded in valid observation and reasoning.

(Please See Chapter 21 Antidotes to Destructive Emotions)

Awareness is the state of perceiving, feeling or
being conscious of events, objects, or sensory patterns...
The process of behavioral change starts with awareness.

(Please See Chapter 5 Awareness)

Believe In Yourself -
At the beginning it may have been hard but now
you've come so far, just continue to have
confidence in yourself.

Benefits of a Sober Lifestyle –

Improved Sleep
Healthier Weight
Better Mental and Emotional Health
Improved Immunity
Lower Risk of Cancer
Reduced Cardiovascular Risk
Improved Memory and Thinking
Feel Better
Look Better
Love Better
Improved Coordination
Have More Money
Worry Less
Passion for Life
Grow Spiritually
Better Relationships
Learn to Love Yourself

Calm is a feeling of inner peace...
staying calm helps you to wisely
respond, rather than thoughtlessly react.

Commitments, of which you have three -
to remain sober...

to maintain your healthy lifestyle...
to continue on your path of happiness and contentment.

(Please See Chapter 7 Your Three Commitments)

Contentment is an emotional state of satisfaction...
being grateful and happy for what you have,
while being patient for what may come...
a state of having accepted your life's circumstances...
a long-term, milder happiness, accompanied by
a stable calmness.

(Please See Chapter 31 Happiness, Contentment
and Inner Peace)

Count your blessings...
be thankful, appreciative and
grateful for the abundance you already have.

Cravings are just thoughts in your head
which hold no power over you, unless you
give them your attention.

(Please See Chapter 12 Cravings)

Determination is the steadfast fortitude you can
draw upon to help you endure,
cope and survive life's challenges and difficulties...
Be determined to continue on your path of
happiness, contentment and an alcohol-free
and healthy lifestyle.

Don't give up on yourself...Ever, Ever, Ever !!!

Emotions, both positive and negative, are just
mental states, messengers that allow you to
direct your attention to the events that
created them...
Do not try to resist them...Listen to them.

(Please See Chapter 20 Emotions - Negative and Positive)

Everything you are looking for, you already have
inside your mind...
happiness, contentment and inner peace.

Exercise - physical activity which helps reduce
anxiety and stress by releasing *feel-good*
hormones...
It improves your overall health and can help
repair some of the damage you've done to your
body processes and brain functions from your
excessive drinking of alcohol...
increases your quality of life...
improves your sleep and
protects against cognitive impairment.

(Please See Chapter 37 The Benefits of Exercise)

Family and **F**riends - show appreciation
for their support and encouragement
throughout your recovery.

Forgiveness:
Forgive *yourself* for all the
bad decisions you've made...
the times you lacked understanding...
your impulsive reactions and behaviors...
the choices you made that caused harm
to others and to yourself.

(Please See Chapter 10 Healing)

Forgive *others,* not because they deserve to be
forgiven but because you need to close
the door to the negativity of your past.

(Please See Chapter 29 Forgiveness)

Generosity is the act of being kind, selfless and giving,
to others as well as to yourself...
increases your well-being and emotional health.

(Please See Chapter 34 Kindness and Generosity)

Gratitude is the quality of being thankful...
the readiness to show appreciation for the
goodness in your life...
appreciating your life as it is right now...
looking at the brighter side of a situation...
savoring life's positive experiences...
taking pleasure in the gifts that you've
been given...
counting all your blessings...
feeling enjoyment and satisfaction from your
current circumstances and not taking things
for granted.

(Please See Chapter 33 Gratitude)

Happiness is a positive and joyful state of
mind...a sense of well-being, with feelings of
satisfaction and fulfillment...
experiencing enjoyment of and
enthusiasm for life.

(Please See Chapter 31 Happiness, Contentment and
Inner Peace)

Healing is the process of making or becoming sound
or healthy again...
Four Things Necessary to Begin Healing –
Be Honest with Yourself
Forgive Yourself
Have Self-Compassion
Start Living in the Present

(Please See Chapter 10 Healing)

Hiking in Nature allows you to savor the
beauty of nature with all your senses,
while benefiting from a whole-body workout.

(Please See Chapter 38 Nature and Hiking in Nature)

Increase your positivity through positive
thinking, positive actions, meditation,
mindfulness and other happiness strategies.

(See Chapter 18 Your Thoughts and Positive Thinking)

Inner Peace is the state of emotional
poise, confidence, calm and inner strength that
you can have in each and every moment.

(Please See Chapter 31 Happiness, Contentment
and Inner Peace)

Judge no one, especially yourself...no good can
come of it.
By practicing mindfulness, you will be non-judgmental.

Kindness is the quality of being friendly, generous,
considerate, gentle, warm and affectionate...
Be kind to others and to yourself.

(Please See Chapter 34 Kindness and Generosity)

Laughter is a happiness strategy...
it helps you to keep a positive and optimistic
attitude, drawing the focus away from any
negative emotions.
Always save room in your day for laughter...
it really is the best medicine.

(Please See Chapter 39 Smiling and Laughing)

Learning is the process of acquiring new
understanding, knowledge, behaviors, skills,
values and attitudes through studying...
Learning is essential for healing and
recovering,
for personal growth and improving emotional health.

(Please See Chapter 36 My Self-Improvement Journey)

Letting Go - Let go of all the things that stop you from
growing and becoming a better person...
all the negativity from your past...
all that makes you weak.

(Please See Chapter 27 Letting Go)

Living in the Present or *the here and now,*
means that you are aware and
mindful of what is happening at *this very moment,*
focused on or centered in *the here and now...*
the only place where life happens.

(Please See Chapter 24 Living in the Present Moment)

Loving-Kindness Meditation - a type of meditation,
where you send out loving thoughts and kind
intentions to yourself, to your loved ones,
to all of humanity.

(Please See Chapter 35 A Loving-Kindness Meditation)

Meditation - is the practice of training your attention
so you can be more aware of your own inner
workings as well as what is happening around you
in the here-and-now.

(Please See Chapter 15 Meditation)

Mindfulness - is your ability to be *Fully Present...*
to be aware of where you are and what

you are doing...
not overreacting...
not judging...
not overwhelmed by what's going on around you.

(Please See Chapter 25 Mindfulness)

Nature - has strong healing properties...
improving your mind...
boosting your immune system...
increasing your positivity...
it can take you out of the prison of
your mind where you might be lost in overthinking,
lost in a complexed maze of self-centered problems
and help you stay focused in the present moment.

(Please See Chapter 38 Nature and Hiking in Nature)

Negativity - a state of being negative...
focusing on what is lacking...
a tendency to be downbeat, disagreeable or
skeptical...
having a pessimistic view of life.

Negativity Bias - also referred to as the
'positive-negative asymmetry' is the tendency
to register negative stimuli more readily than
positive stimuli...
you feel the sting of harsh criticism more powerfully
than the satisfaction of completing a task.

Neural plasticity refers to the *plastic-like*
or *malleable* nature of the brain...
your brain can be *shaped* or *molded*
it can change...
it's the ability of neural networks in the brain
to change through growth and reorganization...
neuron pathways making new connections.

(Please See Chapter 30 Training Your Brain)

Never give up on your commitments...
to remain sober...
to maintain a healthy lifestyle...
to seek happiness and contentment.

(Please See Chapter 7 Your Three Commitments)

Overthinking is thinking too much...
endlessly and excessively contemplating
the meanings, causes and consequences of your
character, your emotions and your problems...
obsessing over something that happened in the past
or fretting over something that may or
may not happen in the future.

(Please See Chapter 22 Overthinking)

Patience is the capacity to accept or
tolerate delay, trouble, or suffering
without getting angry or upset...
The more patient you are, the more accepting
you will be of *what is,* rather than insisting
that life be exactly as you would like it to be.

(Please See Chapter 30 Patience and Tolerance)

Positivity is the state of being positive...
focusing on the good...having a favorable, constructive,
optimistic, confident and upbeat view
of life...leading to happiness.

Qualities - your distinctive attributes or
character traits...
Possessing *Positive Qualities,* such as kindness,
patience and honesty, being grateful, caring, generous,
humble and compassionate...leading to happiness.

(Please See Chapter 16 Your Positive Qualities)

Recovery - a return to a normal state of
health, mind, or strength...
the action or process of regaining
possession or control of something lost...
You do not recover an addiction just by stopping the using...
You recover by creating a new life where it is
easier not to drink alcohol to an excess.
You can fully recover from your AUD

(Please See Chapter 1 You Can and You Will Recover)

Relaxation is the state of being free from
tension and anxiety...
it is an essential part of self-care...
there are many ways to relax, such as spending
some alone-time, reading, writing, singing,
dancing, walking, being in nature.

(Please See Chapter 13 Self-Care)

Repetition - the act of saying something, over and over,
again and again...
By continually repeating positive affirmations,
you can rewire or train your brain towards positivity.

(Please See Chapter 23 Training Your Brain)

Resilience - the capacity to recover quickly from
problematic situations...
the ability to become strong or healthy again after
something bad happens...the capacity to withstand adversity
and rebound from difficult life events.

(Please See Chapter 32 Resilience)

Responsibility is the opportunity or ability to act
independently and make decisions without
authorization... accepting the fact that *you* are the cause and
the solution of the matter...taking care of your own matters
and answering for your own actions...

being accountable for the choices you make.

(Please See Chapter 8 Responsibility and Self-Empowerment)

Rewire or train your brain...
by learning new positive ways of thinking,
you create new neural pathways in your brain...
this creates new positive beliefs and habits...
hardwiring your brain, training your brain
to increase your happiness.

(Please See Chapter 23 Training Your Brain)

Rumination - is a cycle of negative
thinking...
excessive, repetitive thinking about or
dwelling on the same problem or situation.

(Please See Chapter 22 Overthinking)

Savoring refers to the capacity to *attend to, appreciate*
and *enhance* the positive experiences of your life...
to experience something good, *slowly*...
in order for you to enjoy it as much as possible.

(Please See Chapter 28 Slow Down and Savor the Good)

Self-Care is the practice of taking action to preserve or
improve one's own health...
taking an active role in protecting one's own
well-being and happiness...
making a conscious effort to care for your own
physical, mental and emotional health...
taking care of yourself by engaging in
strategies that promote healthy functioning and
enhance your well-being.

(Please See Chapter 13 Self-Care)

Self-Compassion is a form of *acceptance*...

an acceptance of yourself when you are feeling
hurt or pain...
a form of *kindness*...
giving yourself the same kindness that you would
give to someone else that is suffering...
focusing on your desire to be safe...
recognizing that you are deserving of happiness...
it's about having warmth and understanding
towards yourself when you feel inadequate or
feel like a failure.

(Please See Chapter 10 Healing)

Self-Empowerment is taking control of your own life...
setting goals and making positive choices...
making a conscious decision to take charge of
your destiny...
having *self-confidence* (a feeling of trust in your
abilities, qualities and judgment) and then taking
that to the next level, by converting your
intentions into actions.

(Please See Chapter 8 Responsibility and Self-Empowerment)

Self-Improvement is the improvement of
your knowledge or character by your
own efforts...
a personal development of your capabilities and
potential...
with the goal of becoming a better version of yourself.

(Please See Chapter 26 My Self-Improvement Journey)

Slowing Down will make you more aware
of your surroundings...
to see where you are and what is happening...
to be aware of what really matters and what
you really need.

(Please see Chapter 28 Slow Down and Savor the Good)

Smiling is a happiness strategy...
it usually happens as an involuntary response to
something that is bringing you joy or laughter, or
it can be a totally conscious, intentional choice...
your brain doesn't know the difference...
so either way, it makes you look good and
feel marvelous...
and can immediately change your mood, reduce
your stress and anxiety and help you to stay positive.

(Please See Chapter 39 Smiling and Laughing)

Sober Lifestyle - a voluntary choice to live your life
without ever having the need or desire for alcohol.

Stress is a part of life, usually caused by life's
difficulties and challenges...
something you can learn to manage or cope with.

(Please see Chapter 11 Managing Stress)

Support Team - those who supported you
during your recovery...
Thank them for their invaluable support.

(Please See Chapter 17 Your Support Team)

Thoughts are ideas, notions, views or opinions,
produced by thinking, or occurring suddenly
in the mind...
which may or may not be based on reality.

(Please See Chapter 18 Your Thoughts and Positive Thinking)

Tolerance is the ability or willingness to endure,
acknowledge, accept or put up with something,
without interference, in particular, the existence
of opinions or behaviors that you don't necessarily
agree with.

(Please See Chapter 30 Patience and Tolerance)

Training Your Brain - By repeatedly taking in new,
positive information, by focusing on and
remembering positive experiences,
your brain forms new neural pathways,
(the connections in your brain that are
formed based on your habits and behaviors)
which create new positive beliefs and habits...
you are hardwiring your brain...
training your brain to increase your happiness.

(Please See Chapter 23 Training Your Brain)

Understanding - Having understanding towards yourself
is part of self-compassion...
a form of self-acceptance...
sympathetically aware of your own feelings...
tolerant and forgiving of your faults and weaknesses.

(Please See Chapter 10 Healing)

Visualize a better version of yourself...
a happier and healthier you, without the need
or desire for alcohol.

Walking is a low impact exercise which
has benefits for both your mind and your body...
Make it a part of your self-care routine.

X-factor is a noteworthy quality or
talent...
a uniqueness...
something you already have.

Your thoughts are only those thoughts you focus on...
those thoughts which you give your attention to...
You cannot control the thoughts that enter your
brain, but you can choose how to handle them...
You give power only to the thoughts that you

choose to...
They are powerless until you decide to make them
your thoughts.

(Please See Chapter 18 Your Thoughts and Positive Thinking)

Zen - a state of meditative calm or
inner peace...
Do one thing at a time, slowly and deliberately,
completely...
Devote time to sitting...
Smile and serve others...
Think about what is necessary...
Live simply.
Live in the moment.

ABOUT THE AUTHOR

I'm Joey...I'm not an alcoholic!

I was addicted to alcohol...I am not anymore.
Alcohol holds no power over me.
I had an Alcohol Use Disorder...I don't anymore.

Now, I'm a person who chooses not to drink.
I'm a non-drinker...the same as a non-smoker.

Not too long ago, I was an unhappy person...
sad, discouraged and discontent.

In search of refuge from my distress,
I tried distancing myself from the pain...
drowning it out with the temporary,
sensory pleasure from alcohol.

I knew that alcohol would not reverse my
suffering...that it was only a diversion...
It temporarily helped me forget my problems...
did absolutely nothing to solve them and
failed to make me happy.

What it did do was help to slur my speech, lose my
coordination, fall down and on a number of occasions
pass out...
It also made me nasty, obnoxious and not fun
to be around.

I knew I could not continue...I had to put an end
to my alcohol abuse.

When I did stop drinking, I realized I had achieved only
one part of my goal...
Something was still missing from my life.

My ultimate goal was to have a healthy, happy lifestyle,
without the need or desire to drink alcohol...
I didn't want to become an unhappy, sober person.

My focus was on creating a better life for myself ...
If I hadn't accomplished that,
I probably would have returned to drinking.

Today, I can confidently say that I have achieved my goal...

I have Recovered...I am Happy and Content
with No Desire to drink alcohol.

I have just completed my first book, You Have The Power,
to share with you my transformational journey from a
sad and despondent abuser of alcohol to a sober, joyful
and content person with a passion for living.